First published in the United States by
The Lighthouse Academy Press
Printed by Kindle Direct Publishing, USA
Additional copies for sale at Amazon Books

ISBN: 979-8-9995192-4-5

This work was developed through a human–AI collaboration. Draft materials were produced with the assistance of generative tools, after which the author revised, restructured, and refined all text for accuracy, coherence, and fidelity of voice. See *Author's Note*.

The cover and interior images were created using digital rendering tools.

The
Lighthouse
Academy
Press

The Age of the Manufactured Man

*How the Enlightenment Shaped the
Modern Human Condition*

William J. Striker

Contents

Contents

Contents

Contents

for Professor Richard Olson

Harvey Mudd College, Class of 1962

Author's Note

This book was written in a spirit of inquiry rather than judgment. Its aim is not to adjudicate history, but to understand how certain ideas emerged, how they took hold, and how they shaped the modern condition. Others are better suited to render verdicts. This work seeks instead to clarify structure, trace consequence, and restore proportion.

Its composition was supported by collaborative AI tools — used not to write on behalf of the author, but to explore form, clarify structure, and test language against intent. Every passage has been weighed, revised, and refined by the author for coherence, tone, and philosophical clarity. The use of such tools reflects the very subject of the book: the interaction between human judgment and engineered systems, and the necessity of maintaining authorship, responsibility, and intent within that interaction.

No claim is made that the voice behind this work belongs to a single mind. But neither is it impersonal. Every line carries intent. Every page reflects deliberation. The name on the cover is a singular signature, standing for a work shaped through human dialogue, reflection, and choice.

The reader is invited to engage the book in that spirit.

Preface

There are moments in history when familiar words drift loose from their meanings. Concepts that once carried weight through centuries of use become slogans, accusations, or identities, detached from the worlds that gave them coherence.

Our age is rich in vocabulary and poor in memory. It is an unusual combination, and not a harmless one.

Modern political discourse is filled with fragments of older structures: names without architecture, labels without lineage, judgments without history. What is missing is the long view — the awareness that the turmoil of the present is not unique to the present, but part of a much older pattern. From close range, the modern world appears chaotic, unprecedented, and confusing. From a distance, a continuity becomes visible, running across five centuries of Western experience.

This book begins with a simple recognition: modern radicalism — whether expressed in revolution, technocracy, ideological movements, or contemporary theories of the "optimized" human — is a direct legacy of the Enlightenment. Enabled by the Reformation and the Scientific Revolution, a new conception of the human being emerged in the West: **the belief that human nature is malleable**, that society functions as a mechanism, and that both may be reshaped through rational design.

This is the hinge upon which the modern age pivots.

Ancient and medieval societies largely assumed a fixed human nature within an inherited order of meaning. Modern societies did not. Once human nature came to be regarded as improvable — indeed, as *makeable* — politics changed its character. It ceased to be primarily the art of governing human beings as they are and became increasingly the project of remaking human beings according to an ideal. Modern radical movements, whether violent or administrative, revolutionary or therapeutic, arise from this conviction. They are not merely political. They are anthropological. These movements differ in method, temperament, and moral tone, yet they share a common inheritance. They are branches from the same trunk.

Much of the commentary available today suffers from two persistent defects. The first is short-term vision: a fixation on personalities, elections, and immediate controversies. The second is conceptual amnesia: the assumption that our political categories have always existed in their present form. Neither is sufficient for understanding the world we inhabit. The result is a public culture that speaks confidently about structures it no longer recognizes, using the vocabulary of the past to describe conditions of the present.

The purpose of this book is to recover a long arc — to explain modern radicalism and autocracy not as reactions to particular events or personalities, but as the outcome of an intellectual transformation that began five centuries ago. The Enlightenment, often celebrated for its contributions to liberty and reason, also introduced a new anthropology: man as improvable material. Once human nature was treated as something that might be engineered, politics expanded from governance into redesign.

This book does not argue that this transformation was a mistake, nor does it imagine that its consequences can — or should — be undone. Much of modern life has been genuinely improved by the very developments examined here. Disease has been reduced, material suffering eased, knowledge expanded, and opportunity widened. The genie cannot be put back in the bottle, nor does this work suggest that it should be.

What it does suggest is that something was gained — and something was lost.

This volume does not offer a grand unifying theory of history. Human history resists such efforts. It is too rich, too contingent, and too various to be captured by a single explanatory system. But history can be understood through perspectives — through threads traced across a larger tapestry. This book follows one such thread: the belief in human makeability — its expansion, its consequences, and the limits it eventually encounters.

The aim is not alarm, but proportion. Not judgment, but understanding. If the reader emerges with a clearer sense of how modern society came to believe that the human being is something to be redesigned, and how that belief continues to shape our age, then the book will have served the purpose for which it was written.

The Age of the
Manufactured Man

Introduction

Modern politics appears chaotic because we stand too close to it. The turbulence of the moment — its movements, counter-movements, anxieties, and demands — presents itself as something unprecedented. Yet step back, even a little, and the disorder begins to resolve. What seemed like fragmentation reveals itself as continuity. The noise gives way to pattern that stretches across centuries.

That pattern rests upon a simple but revolutionary idea: **human nature can be shaped**.

This idea would have been unintelligible to the ancient world. The Greeks understood man within a natural order; the Romans within tradition and inheritance; the Middle Ages within a divine framework. Even the most absolute rulers — Alexander, Augustus, Qin Shi Huang — sought obedience, not transformation. They governed men as they were. They did not attempt to remake them.

Then came the Enlightenment.

In the wake of the Reformation and the Scientific Revolution, the West began to see both nature and man differently. If nature could be reduced to laws, analyzed, and improved, then society might be approached in the same way. If institutions were human constructions rather than sacred inheritances, they could be redesigned. And if reason and education could elevate the mind, then the human being itself might become an object of deliberate improvement.

Once human nature became *makeable*, the political world entered a new course.

The movements that followed — Jacobinism, Bolshevism, Maoism, scientific management, eugenics, technocracy — did not limit themselves to reform. They aimed at reconstruction. Society was no longer something to be governed; it was something to be engineered. The citizen was no longer simply a participant; he became a subject of improvement. Disagreement was not merely opposition; it appeared as error to be corrected. Politics, increasingly, assumed the character of therapy.

This is the defining feature of modern radicalism. It is not political in the classical sense; it is *therapeutic*. It proceeds as though the human condition itself were a problem to be solved.

Without recognizing this shift, the modern world appears as a collection of disconnected phenomena — ideological revolutions, autocratic regimes, social movements, technological utopianism, cultural reeducation, and algorithmic influence. With it, these developments take on a different character. They become expressions of a single transformation unfolding over time.

This book examines that transformation through two related ideas.

First, the **makeable man** as a belief: the conviction, emerging in the eighteenth century, that human nature is open to improvement, redesign, and correction. This belief begins as philosophy, moves into policy, and ultimately becomes practice.

Second, the **manufactured man** as the result: taking root in the mid-20th century, the condition that arises when societies possess not only the belief in human malleability, but also the tools, institutions, and techniques to produce it — continuously, at scale, and increasingly from within.

We therefore inhabit two overlapping ages: the age of the makeable man, now several centuries old; and the age of the manufactured man, a more recent development, but one already shaping daily life. The earlier chapters trace the emergence of the idea. The later chapters examine the lived condition.

The narrative follows this lineage from its Enlightenment origins through its successive expressions. It considers how movements grounded in reason sought to rebuild society, and how efforts to improve the human condition gave rise to new forms of control — sometimes overt, sometimes subtle. It also addresses the growing incoherence of modern political language, whose terms have become detached from their historical foundations.

The purpose is not to advocate a return to an earlier age, nor to condemn the impulse toward improvement. It is to restore clarity. By reconnecting present conditions to their origins, the modern world becomes more intelligible — not a collection of crises, but the unfolding of ideas long in motion.

Clarity restores proportion.

Proportion restores understanding.

Understanding restores the long view.

And with it, the age appears not as chaos, but as continuity.

Part I:
Before the Age of the
Makeable Human

Chapter 1
The Given Human

For most of human history, the question of what a human being is was not a matter for debate. It was treated as settled — as settled as the rising of the sun or the turning of the seasons.

Human nature was not considered a raw material to be molded, still less a project to be redesigned. It was *given*. One could refine character, elevate conduct, or pursue wisdom, but the essential nature of man was fixed, stable, reliable. He was not something to be engineered, but something to be understood.

The societies of the ancient world — Greek, Roman, Persian, Egyptian, Chinese, and Indian — disagreed about many things: gods, politics, the good life, the structure of society. But they shared one conviction: the human being is not infinitely pliable.

The Greeks grounded humanity in reason and nature. The Romans anchored it in tradition, law, and virtue. The Chinese embedded it in ritual and harmony. The medieval world saw it as divinely made and morally accountable. Across cultures, across centuries, the common thread was continuity. Man had a nature, and society built around it.

As Aristotle[1] observed, the state itself arises from nature, not invention, and man is by nature a political animal.

Even the most innovative societies of the ancient world did not imagine that human nature could be remade. The Athenians transformed the relations of man to man — inventing the citizen, the assembly, the jury, and equality before the law — but they never believed they could transform man himself.

---

[1] Aristotle, *Politics*, Book I, 1253a. Jowett translation (Oxford, 1885): "Hence it is evident that the state is a creation of nature, and that man is by nature a political animal."

In Greek myth, the gods change forms but never natures. Daphne becomes a laurel, Io a cow, Callisto a bear — yet their identities persist. Transformation alters appearance, not essence. The self remains intact.

The cosmos placed boundaries.

This conviction arose from a deeper source than politics. The ancient world assumed a structure to existence: a natural order in Greece; a moral order in Rome; a cosmic justice in Persia; a harmony in China; a divine purpose in medieval Europe.

These systems differed in detail, but all understood human nature as part of an existing architecture. The human being was not an invention but an inheritance — part of a world already given shape by gods, laws, nature, or Heaven.

This gave ancient political life a certain stability. No matter how violent, corrupt, or unjust a regime became, its ambitions remained bounded. Political systems could rise and fall, but they did not imagine themselves capable of crafting new souls.

The ancient political imagination had limits.

Shah Abbas reorganized Persia, building armies and administrations, but the nature of the subject remained untouched.

Qin Shi Huang unified China with iron discipline and reshaped the institutions of the empire, yet even he did not imagine that he could remake human consciousness.

Ancient rulers altered laws, borders, and obligations — but not the essence of the human being.

Even Alexander the Great, whose empire spanned continents, refrained from imposing new customs on the peoples he conquered. He ruled within the inherited order; he did not imagine he could redesign the human being.

A Roman emperor could be monstrous — Caligula proved that — but even he did not conceive of transforming Roman citizens into a new kind of being. His maxim, according to

Suetonius, was simple: "Let them hate me, so long as they fear me." He demanded loyalty, not rebirth. [2]

A medieval king could be cruel, but he ruled within a cosmology that stood above him. He did not attempt to replace that cosmology with one of his own design.

Charlemagne, the greatest ruler of the early Middle Ages, governed within the world as he found it. Einhard tells us that when he examined the legal systems of his peoples, he did not seek to replace them, but to "add what was lacking, to reconcile the differences, and to amend anything that was wrong or wrongly expressed." He even ordered that the traditional laws of all the nations under his rule be collected and committed to writing — not rewritten according to a new design. [3]

His authority worked with inherited structures, not against them. In Charlemagne's world, the aim was correction, not creation; preservation, not reinvention.

Human nature was not the object of political power. It was the backdrop against which power operated.

What the ancient world never conceived — the remaking of man — would become the defining ambition of the modern one.

---

[2] "Oderint dum metuant" from *The Lives of the Twelve Caesars*, by C. Suetonius Tranquillus, §30 (c. AD 121).

[3] Einhard, *Vita Karoli Magni,* Ch. 29 (Grant translation). Einhard was a Frankish scholar and courtier in service of Charlemagne and his son, Louis the Pios.

Chapter 2
The Harmony of Inheritance

To understand what changed in the modern age, it is necessary to understand what held the ancient world together.

Before the Enlightenment transformed the relationship between man and the world, human beings lived within an inherited order — not by choice, but by condition. Meaning was not constructed; it was received. This inheritance shaped the way people lived, worshiped, worked, married, fought, and ruled. It formed the outer boundary of political imagination and the inner boundary of personal identity.

Every civilization articulated this inheritance differently, yet all understood it as something older and wiser than any individual will. The world had a shape before one arrived. The task was not to invent a structure of meaning, but to align oneself with the one already present. Ancient political life operated within a metaphysical frame that no ruler, no reformer, and no assembly believed they could overturn.

In Greece, the lawful order — *nomos* — was understood as a balance between *physis* (nature) and human reason. Life made sense when lived in accordance with both. The citizen belonged to the *polis*, and the *polis* existed within a cosmos governed by intelligible principles.

In Rome, tradition — *mos maiorum* — served as a stabilizing force that preserved virtue and duty across generations. Roman law evolved, but always as a continuation of what had been received, never as an attempt to replace the nature of man.

In China, harmony — *he* — was the universal ideal: an alignment of Heaven, Earth, and humanity. Ritual rooted human activity in patterns far older than any dynasty, reminding each person of their place within a cosmic order.

In India, the cosmic law — *dharma* — provided a moral and spiritual framework that connected the individual to the universe and governed duty through caste, family, and role.

In the medieval world, divine purpose established the moral architecture of life; even kings bent to its authority.

To modern readers, these systems may appear restrictive or rigid. Yet they offered a remarkable compensation: they placed boundaries around human ambition. They made it clear that man was not sovereign over the world, and certainly not sovereign over human nature. The ruler's reach was wide, but his domain did not include the soul. Transformation belonged to gods, not to men — and even the gods in myth could change form, but not essence.

Inheritance, in this older world, was more than property or custom. It was a philosophy of existence. It reminded every generation that order was not manufactured, but found; that meaning preceded action; that the world possessed a logic of its own before one's birth and would retain it long after one's death.

This inheritance also created continuity.

A Roman citizen understood the virtues expected of him because they had been modeled for centuries. A Chinese villager performed rituals whose origins he could not fully explain, but whose coherence he could feel. An Athenian juror understood that justice was not his invention; it was a participation in a structure of justice — *dike* — older than the city itself.

Even political upheavals — wars, usurpations, conquests — unfolded within this older architecture. A king might replace another, but the nature of the king, the role of the subject, and the moral expectations upon both remained intact. Politics rearranged society, but it did not attempt to reconfigure humanity.

When, in 522 BC, the Persian conspirators overthrew the Magian usurper and debated whether Persia should be ruled by one, by a few, or by many, they were not debating the nature of man. They were debating who should rule and how — not what a human being is. Across Greece, Rome, China, and Persia, political change reshaped hierarchy and administration, but left the deeper structure of humanity untouched.

Ancient reform assumed the nature of man to be fixed; it reorganized society in accordance with it.

The harmony of inheritance did not eliminate suffering or injustice. Ancient life could be harsh, hierarchical, and at times cruel. But even its cruelty was bounded by a metaphysical frame that made total transformation unthinkable. The idea that human nature itself could be redesigned — that the self could be engineered — had no place in this worldview.

This is the forgotten inheritance of the pre-Enlightenment world: a world in which being preceded making, and meaning stood deeper than intention.

It formed the stage upon which the modern age would perform its great reversal.

Part II:
The Revolution in Thought
(1500 – 1800)

Chapter 3
The Reformation and
the Collapse of the Sacred Canopy

For more than a thousand years, Europe lived beneath a unified metaphysical architecture. The Church — for all its failings — provided a single interpretive framework: a common doctrine, a common calendar, a common moral universe, and a shared understanding of salvation and authority. From Ireland to Sicily, from the Baltic to Spain, an English peasant and a Venetian merchant inhabited the same story of the world.

This structure did not merely regulate belief. It organized time in the liturgical year, community in the parish, death in the rites of burial, and the legitimacy of marriage, law, and kingship. Kings ruled by the grace of God; commoners lived within a moral hierarchy older than any kingdom.

This was the sacred canopy of medieval Europe: a unifying order understood to descend from Heaven.

The fracture begins in 1517, when Martin Luther posted his Ninety-Five Theses, he intended to challenge corruption — not metaphysics. Yet his insistence on *sola fide* and *sola scriptura*[4] cut deeper than the indulgence trade.[5] It challenged the Church's

---

[4] *Sola fide* ("faith alone") and *sola scriptura* ("Scripture alone") were central Reformation doctrines. They held that salvation is attained through faith rather than works, and that Scripture, rather than Church authority or tradition, is the sole source of religious truth.

[5] Indulgences were certificates issued by Church authorities promising remission of temporal punishment for sins. In late medieval Europe, they became formalized documents — often elaborately sealed — that could be purchased to reduce time in purgatory for oneself or for departed relatives. Their commercialization, especially by the Dominican friar Johann Tetzel, provoked widespread resentment and was a direct catalyst for Luther's protest in 1517.

17

role as the mediator of truth. If salvation comes by faith alone, and if Scripture interprets itself, then the believer stands before God without priest, sacrament, or hierarchy.

This shifted the axis of meaning.

Authority no longer descended from a single center. It moved inward — toward individual conscience.

Without Gutenberg's press, Luther might have remained an obscure monk. With it, his tracts spread across Europe in weeks. By 1520, Lutheran pamphlets had reached England, Bohemia, Scandinavia, and parts of Italy — far beyond the reach of any single ecclesiastical authority to contain or correct them. The speed mattered. Ideas now moved faster than institutions could respond.

The printing press did not merely multiply texts; it reorganized authority.

Religious legitimacy began to shift from office to circulation. Bishops and councils no longer monopolized interpretation when printed arguments could be read, copied, and debated by anyone with access to a pamphlet. Scripture and doctrine were no longer encountered primarily through mediated instruction, but through private reading and communal discussion. Interpretation moved outward, from institution to reader.

This produced something unprecedented in European life: durable disagreement.

Competing doctrines could coexist in print. Suppressed ideas did not disappear; they resurfaced elsewhere, unchanged. Retractions were ineffective once copies had spread. Orthodoxy could no longer be restored by decree alone, because authority itself had fractured.

What emerged were not simply new opinions, but parallel structures of allegiance — communities bound not by geography or hierarchy, but by shared texts and shared interpretations. Meaning no longer operated under a single canopy. It splintered, accelerated, and moved beyond the control of those who had previously governed it.

Once interpretation escaped the cathedral, fragmentation was inevitable.

Lutherans in Germany, Calvinists in France and Switzerland, Zwinglians in Zurich, Anabaptists in the German states, Anglicans in England, Hussites and later Unitarians in Bohemia, Puritans in England and New England — each claimed access to divine truth, each claimed Scriptural legitimacy, each claimed conscience as authority. But these consciences did not agree.

Europe fractured into theological worlds that no longer recognized one another.

The collapse of the sacred canopy produced a century of conflict. The German Peasants' War, the French Wars of Religion, the Dutch Revolt, the St. Bartholomew's Day Massacre, the Thirty Years' War, and the English Civil War were not merely political struggles. They were crises of meaning — battles between incompatible visions of the human soul.

The Peace of Westphalia in 1648 concluded this period by granting princes the right to determine religion within their territories.[6] But the deeper unity was gone. A world that had shared a single story now contained many, none of which could claim unquestioned authority.

The Reformation did not promote nihilism. It was an attempt to recover purity and fidelity. Yet in shattering the old unity, it redirected the structure of meaning: from institution to individual, from inherited order to interpretive freedom, from given meaning to discerned meaning.

The believer now bore responsibilities once carried by the Church — to interpret the world, to define conscience, to locate

---

[6] *Cuius regio, eius religio* — "whose realm, his religion" meaning that the religion of the ruler was to dictate the religion of those ruled.

authority. This inward turn altered the relationship between man and meaning.

With no single authority to adjudicate doctrine, the self became the final court of appeal.

This was not yet the modern project of remaking man. But it created a new possibility.

If meaning can be interpreted, perhaps it can be adjusted.

If it can be adjusted, perhaps it can be constructed.

If constructed, perhaps it can be designed.

If designed, perhaps man himself can be redesigned.

The Enlightenment would take the next step. Where the Reformation placed meaning in individual conscience, the Enlightenment placed it in the human mind — the rational, designing faculty.

The Reformation fractured the sacred canopy. The Enlightenment replaced the sky.

The modern age begins here — not with the intention to remake man, but with the collapse of the world in which man was given.

Chapter 4
The Scientific Revolution and the Mechanization of Nature

Interpretation, no longer unified, moved inward to individual conscience. The Scientific Revolution of the seventeenth century altered something deeper: the relationship between man and the world.

Where the medieval mind saw nature as symbolic, sacramental, and alive with purpose, the new thinkers of Europe began to see it differently: a mechanism governed by laws — intelligible, predictable, and open to mastery.

This was not merely a shift in method. It was a shift in metaphysics.

Francis Bacon urged Europe to abandon scholastic speculation and turn to observation, experiment, and induction. His call for a *new instrument* — *Novum Organum* — was not a stylistic flourish, but a philosophical reorientation. Nature, he argued, is not a field of symbols; it is a field of causes and effects, discoverable through method.

In place of contemplation, Bacon offered investigation. In place of submission, interrogation. In place of inherited meaning, useful knowledge.

His blunt formula made the point without ambiguity: knowledge is power. [7] He meant it literally. Where causes are known, effects can be produced; where the course of nature is

---

[7] Francis Bacon, *Novum Organum*, Aphorism 3 (1620).
See also Will Durant, *The Age of Reason Begins*, chap. VII, "The Summons to Reason," for discussion of Bacon's motto *ipsa scientia potestus est* ("knowledge itself is power").

understood, it can be directed. Nature, to be commanded, must be obeyed.

Bacon did not claim to remake nature. But he implied that once understood, it could be worked upon — treated, in effect, as material.

René Descartes pressed the logic further. In *Principles of Philosophy*, he described matter as extension in motion — a vast kinetic geometry intelligible through mathematics. Animals, he argued, were automata: complex machines composed of moving parts.

The implications were immediate:
> Nature possessed no intrinsic purpose.
> Only laws, motion, and mechanism remained.
> To understand was to predict; to predict was to control.

Descartes' vision was not malicious. But its consequence was profound. If nature is mechanism, then mastery is not arrogance — it is method.

Isaac Newton completed the transformation. The *Principia* did not merely provide equations; it supplied a new picture of reality. The same force that moves an apple governs the planets. The same mathematics that traces an orbit describes tides, comets, and trajectories.

In one stroke, the heavens ceased to be symbolic, and nature ceased to be mysterious. The cosmos became a unified system governed by universal laws.

Newton's universe did not require continuous intervention. It required understanding. And once understood, it could be calculated, predicted, and — within limits — directed.

No earlier civilization had imagined such a world.

From these developments, a new posture toward reality emerged. Knowledge was no longer alignment with an inherited order; it became an instrument for reshaping the world. Nature was no longer a partner in existence; it became, increasingly, material.

A new figure appeared — not the priest, not the philosopher, not the sage, but the engineer: the one who applies knowledge to design, construct, optimize, and improve.

For millennia, nature had set the terms. Now, man could begin to set them.

This shift was not yet directed toward the human being. Bacon did not propose to reconstruct human nature. Descartes did not outline a program for redesigning the self. Newton did not imagine the psyche as an object of engineering.

But together they created a framework in which such ambitions became thinkable.

Once nature was intelligible through universal laws, the next questions followed with quiet inevitability:

If the world is a mechanism, why not society?

If society, why not the mind?

If the mind, why not man himself?

The transformation was not immediate, but the pattern was set.

The metaphysics of mechanism prepared the ground for the perfectibility of man — a project the Enlightenment would embrace with increasing confidence.

The Scientific Revolution did not manufacture man. But it taught Europe to see the world as something that could be manufactured. And in that change of vision lay the seeds of everything that followed.

Chapter 5
The Enlightenment and the Birth of the Perfectible Human

The Scientific Revolution taught Europe to see the world as a mechanism governed by law — intelligible, measurable, and open to mastery. The Enlightenment extended this attitude from nature to man, beginning in the late seventeenth century and reaching its peak in the eighteenth. It proposed that human nature, like the physical universe, might be understood, improved, and perhaps even redesigned.

For millennia, civilizations had treated human nature as fixed — a given of the world. The Enlightenment broke from this inheritance. It suggested that human beings are not passive recipients of a predetermined order, but active participants in the construction of a better future. In the hands of the *philosophes*, human nature itself became material for reform.

The confidence in reason was more than intellectual optimism. It was a new anthropology. Reason could diagnose the defects of society and prescribe their cure. Custom, tradition, and inherited forms were no longer stabilizing forces; they became obstacles to progress.

Authority, once grounded in divine command or ancestral wisdom, now resided in human rationality.
What could be understood could be corrected.
What could be corrected could be improved.
What could be improved might be perfected.

Jean-Jacques Rousseau stands at the center of this transformation. In the *Discourse on Inequality*, *The Social Contract*, and *Émile*, he rejected the ancient assumption of a stable human nature. Man, he argued, is naturally good; it is society — its conventions, hierarchies, and institutions — that corrupts him.

If this is so, then the defects of man are not permanent. They are circumstantial.

Change the circumstances, and the man may be changed.

As Rousseau wrote at the opening of *The Social Contract*: "Man is born free, and everywhere he is in chains."[8] The chains were not natural; they were constructed — and therefore could be removed or remade.

Rousseau's distinction between natural man and civil man marks a decisive step. Natural man is whole, independent, and instinctual. Civil man is formed — shaped by law, custom, and political will. He is not merely educated; he is constituted.

For the first time, the contrast becomes explicit:

Man as he is by nature

versus

Man as he might be under a redesigned political order

No ancient thinker would have recognized the distinction.

In *Émile*, Rousseau provides a blueprint for moral formation. "Everything is good as it leaves the hands of the Author of things; everything degenerates in the hands of man."[9] If society corrupts, then society must be rebuilt. If institutions deform, they must be reimagined. If education shapes the soul, then the soul may be shaped deliberately.

Human nature is no longer destiny. It becomes design.

Rousseau's most consequential claim lies deeper still. The individual, he argued, is not the final judge of his own good. The sovereign — the general will — determines what the citizen truly wants, even when he does not recognize it.

His formulation is as stark as it is enduring: "Whoever refuses to obey the general will shall be compelled to do so by

---

[8] Rousseau, *The Social Contract*, Book I, ch. 1 (1762).
[9] Rousseau, Émile, Book I (1762).

the whole body; this means nothing less than that he will be forced to be free." [10]

Here appears the seed of a new kind of authority: one that claims to know the individual better than he knows himself, to reshape him for his own good, and to justify coercion in the name of moral progress.

This is not yet the guillotine. But it is the idea behind the guillotine.

Nicolas de Condorcet extended the doctrine of perfectibility into history itself. In his *Sketch for a Historical Picture of the Progress of the Human Mind*, he argued that reason advances without limit, that knowledge expands cumulatively, and that moral improvement follows in its wake.

History acquires direction. Progress becomes a secular providence.

Condorcet wrote these words while in hiding from the Jacobins who would soon condemn him. His optimism survived the circumstances that refuted it.

Once history is understood to move toward improvement, the logic follows:

> Human reason advances without limit.
> Knowledge grows cumulatively.
> Moral improvement follows.
> Therefore progress has no inherent boundary.
> Ends begin to justify means. Transformation becomes not only possible, but necessary.

Denis Diderot and d'Alembert's *Encyclopédie* gathered the arts and sciences into a single work — not as a museum, but as a manual. Its purpose was emancipatory: to free mankind from ignorance and superstition by making knowledge available as a tool.

Knowledge becomes construction material.

---

[10] Rousseau, The *Social Contract*, Book I, ch. 7 (1762).

If institutions are human constructs, they may be rebuilt. If character is formed by institutions, it may be reshaped.

The Enlightenment thus transforms human nature from inheritance into project.

By its close, a new anthropology has taken hold:

> Human nature is malleable.
> Institutions shape man.
> Reason can redesign institutions.
> Therefore reason can redesign man.
> Progress has no inherent limit.
> History has direction.
> The individual is not the final judge of his own good.

This is not yet the makeable man in his modern form.

But it is the architecture into which he will be built.

The question has shifted.

Not: how should man live within the order of the world?

But: how might the world be redesigned so that man becomes what he ought to be?

Once that question is opened, the trajectory is set.

The age of the perfectible human begins its movement toward the age of the manufactured one.

Chapter 6
The Jacobins and the First Attempt at Re-Engineering Man

By the late eighteenth century, the intellectual architecture for the makeable human had been assembled:

> Human nature is malleable.
> Institutions shape the citizen.
> Reason can redesign institutions.
> Therefore reason can redesign man.
> Progress has direction.
> History has meaning.
> The individual is not the final judge of his own good.

All that remained was someone willing to try. The French Revolution provided the stage. The Jacobins supplied the will.

The Reign of Terror (1793–1794) was not merely a political convulsion. It was the first deliberate attempt in Western history to transform human nature through the instruments of the state. It was an experiment — conscious, articulate, and ruthless — in manufacturing a new kind of citizen.

Under Robespierre and Saint-Just, the revolutionaries held that the defects of mankind were not permanent traits, but the products of corrupt institutions. Remove the old order, they argued, and regenerate the human being. A new moral world was not only possible — it was obligatory.

Rousseau had written that the general will might compel the individual "to be free".[11]

---

[11] Jean-Jacques Rousseau, *The Social Contract* (1762), Book I, Chapter 7 ("The Sovereign"): In order then that the social compact may not be an empty formula, it tacitly includes the undertaking … that whoever refuses to obey the general will shall be compelled to do so by the whole body. This means nothing less than that he will be forced to be free … (*on le forcera d'être libre*). Trans. G.D.H. Cole.

The Jacobins made this an administrative principle.

Those who resisted regeneration did not merely oppose a faction; they opposed virtue itself. And virtue, in the Jacobin mind, was inseparable from public reason. To disagree was not to dissent; it was to demonstrate corruption.

Saint-Just declared: "You have done nothing for liberty if you do not annihilate everything that can stand in your way." [12] This was not hyperbole. It was policy. For him, annihilation was not a metaphor; it was the necessary completion of liberty.

The Jacobins treated society as a system to be purified and rebuilt.

The calendar was redesigned to erase Christian memory.

Festivals were invented to cultivate civic virtue.

Language was policed to eliminate inherited distinctions.

Surveillance committees enforced moral rectitude.

Education was recast as the formation of republican character.

Religion was replaced with the Cult of Reason, and later the Cult of the Supreme Being.

None of these were accidents or excesses. They were the logical expression of Enlightenment perfectibility.

If reason can redesign institutions, and institutions shape man, then man is reconfigurable.

If the citizen deviates from virtue, society must correct him.

If society is the source of corruption, it must be purified.

If human nature is improvable, improvement becomes mandatory.

This was the first application of moral engineering at state scale.

In the classical world, tyranny was political — it sought obedience. The Jacobins transformed coercion into moral purification.

---

[12] Louis Antoine de Saint-Just, *Discours sur Louis XVI*, Convention nationale, 13 décembre 1792: "Vous n'avez rien fait pour la liberté si vous n'anéantissez tout ce qui peut vous faire obstacle."

Terror became therapeutic.

Robespierre described it as "nothing other than prompt, severe, inflexible justice; it is therefore an emanation of virtue."[13] In that sentence lies the first explicit justification for using coercive violence to redeem human nature.

Force was no longer merely a means of securing power. It became a means of creating the regenerated human.

The Jacobins attempted what no ancient or medieval order had conceived: to erase inherited identity, to replace it with civic identity, and to enforce that identity with the instruments of the state.

The citizen was no longer a legal status.
He became an anthropological project — defined by virtue, reason, and loyalty to the general will.

Human beings were to be made, not merely ruled.

The Terror collapsed under the weight of its own unbearable purity. Within months, the architects of regeneration became its final victims.

Saint-Just — who had demanded the annihilation of everything that opposed the Republic — was guillotined at twenty-six, executed by the Convention he had once commanded with icy certainty. Robespierre, unable to bear arrest, attempted suicide; the wound shattered his jaw, and when the executioner tore away the bandage on the scaffold, he uttered a single scream before the blade fell.

The machinery they had built consumed its engineers.

Before the Thermidorian reaction[14] ended the experiment, the revolutionary government had executed roughly twenty

---

[13] Robespierre, "Sur les principes de morale politique", speech to the National Convention, 5 février 1794 (17 pluviôse an II), in *Œuvres de Robespierre*, ed. A. Vermorel (Paris: F. Cournol, 1866), 294–308. The original sentence reads: « La terreur n'est autre chose que la justice prompte, sévère, inflexible; elle est donc une émanation de la vertu. ».

[14] The Thermidorian Reaction (9 Thermidor, Year II; July 27, 1794) marks the fall of Maximilien Robespierre, when growing fear and self-

thousand people under state authority — two thousand in Paris by the blade, the rest across the provinces by firing squads, military commissions, drownings, and tribunal carts. [15] The drownings at Nantes were the most indiscriminate: men, women, children, nuns, refractory priests, and peasants loaded into scuttled boats and left to the Loire. [16]

This was purification by elimination.

Yet the idea did not die.

The Jacobins demonstrated something unprecedented: that a modern state, armed with an ideal of perfectibility and a philosophy of human re-creation, could attempt to manufacture virtue by redesigning society itself.

Their project failed. Its logic survived.

In the Bolshevik New Soviet Man.

In Maoist thought reform.

In the administrative utopias of technocracy.

In the subtle behavioral architectures of the digital age.

The Jacobins offered the world the first blueprint for the manufactured citizen. They were the first to walk through the door the Enlightenment had opened.

In doing so, they inaugurated the modern age of radical transformation — the belief that man can be remade for the sake of an ideal.

---

preservation within the revolutionary leadership redirected the Terror against its own authors, bringing its radical phase to an end.

[15] The "tribunal carts" were the tumbrils — wooden wagons used by the Revolutionary Tribunal to transport condemned prisoners from the Conciergerie to the Place de la Révolution for execution. The carts formed part of the visible machinery of the Terror: a public procession carrying the convicted from judgment to the guillotine, transforming death into a ritual of civic purification.

[16] Jean-Baptiste Carrier, the Representative-on-Mission tasked with suppressing the Vendéan rebellion, oversaw the mass drownings in the Loire. He referred to them as "baptêmes républicains" — republican baptisms — a grim euphemism capturing the belief that the Republic purified itself through elimination.

Part III:
The Engineering Age
(1800 – 1950)

Chapter 7
Utopian Socialists and the Prototype Human

By the early nineteenth century, the intellectual ground of Europe had shifted decisively. The old metaphysical order had collapsed, yet the revolutionary alternative had failed to sustain moral coherence. What remained was not only political instability, but an open question about the nature of society itself.

Into this space stepped a group of thinkers who neither sought restoration nor further convulsion. They proposed something new: that society could be deliberately designed, and that through its design the human being could be remade.

With them, the Enlightenment's abstract belief in human malleability took on a concrete, secular form.

Europe stood between two exhausted worlds: the ancien régime, [17] whose architecture had given way, and the Revolution, which had burned fiercely but left no stable order in its wake. From this interval emerged a new ambition — not to govern wisely, but to construct.

A new figure appeared: not the reformer, not the revolutionary, but the designer of society.

Saint-Simon, Fourier, and Owen rejected terror. They rejected the guillotine's promise to regenerate man by punishment. Their ambition was greater — and more modern.

---

[17] "Ancien régime" refers to the pre-Revolutionary social and political order of France, characterized by hereditary monarchy, aristocratic privilege, and the interwoven authority of crown and church. In a broader sense, historians use the term to describe the traditional hierarchies and inherited structures of European society prior to 1789.

They sought a prototype human: a being whose character, passions, morals, and destiny were no longer inherited, but constructed.

Claude-Henri de Saint-Simon emerged from the wreckage of the Revolution convinced that the old order had perished and that a new one must be consciously designed.

He argued:

> Politics must yield to administration.
> Priests must yield to scientists.
> Society must become a coordinated system of production.
> The purpose of that system is the moral elevation of mankind.

This was, once again, radically new. The state was no longer the guardian of inherited order; it became the manager of human development.

Humanity, he insisted, proceeds through stages. It can be raised — step by step — like a child guided by tutors.

Saint-Simon's followers would later produce both technocracy and Marxism — one seeking salvation through experts, the other through history. In both cases, man becomes material. [18]

The Saint-Simonians elevated society itself to a kind of secular divinity, a higher order toward which human life should be directed. In doing so, they inaugurated a project that would define the next two centuries: the replacement of Providence with planning.

If Saint-Simon conceived the system, Charles Fourier redesigned the human within it. [19]

---

[18] For a sympathetic but critical treatment of Saint-Simonian "religion", see Durant's discussion of Comte's *Religion of Humanity* in *The Story of Philosophy*, ch. VIII, "Herbert Spencer"; and Frank E. Manuel, *The Prophets of Paris*, chs. 2–3.

[19] Charles Fourier (1772–1837), the French utopian socialist, should not be confused with Jean-Baptiste Joseph Fourier (1768–1830), the mathematician and physicist.

No thinker before him attempted a more systematic reconstruction of human nature. The passions, he believed, were not obstacles, but raw materials. The existing order mutilated them; a properly designed environment would harmonize them.

His answer was the *phalanstery* — part monastery, part laboratory — in which every passion would find its appointed outlet. He quantified them, categorized them, and assigned them economic and erotic functions.

It was the first attempt to map the human soul for administrative use.

The Enlightenment had claimed that man is malleable. Fourier accepted the claim — and designed a machine to do the molding.

His vision stands behind later attempts to harmonize personality through structure: the commune, the total institution, the behavioral program, and, in our own age, the digital feedback architecture that shapes habit without our awareness.

Of the utopian socialists, Robert Owen was the most practical — and the most confident.

Where Saint-Simon theorized and Fourier schematized, Owen built. At New Lanark, he constructed a community intended to manufacture not goods, but character. He redesigned work rhythms, education, incentives, and the daily texture of life itself.

His conclusion was stated with disarming clarity: "Character is formed by circumstances."

Here the Enlightenment's latent premise becomes doctrine:
> If character is formed by circumstances,
> and if circumstances can be designed,
> then character can be designed.

Owen believed this could be done peacefully, benevolently, scientifically. He attempted it in Scotland and again in America. His communities failed.

The conviction did not.

It endured as a new commonplace: that society can produce the kind of human being it desires.

The utopian socialists were not radicals in the political sense. They sought no barricades and shed no blood. They denounced the Jacobins rather than imitated them.

But in intellectual history, they were more revolutionary.

For the first time in secular form, they proposed:

> Man is improvable without inherent limit.
> Institutions are tools for shaping the human being.
> A new social architecture can produce a new moral species.
> The defects of mankind are not innate, but the residue of obsolete structures.

They were the first real engineers of the human future.

Every movement that followed — from Marxism to managerial progressivism, from technocracy to psychological conditioning, from eugenics to algorithmic nudging — begins here.

Saint-Simon, Fourier, and Owen did not build the machinery of modern radicalism. They produced its blueprints.

They taught the modern world to imagine that human nature could be not merely guided — but redesigned.

Thus begins the Age of the Manufactured Man. Not in terror. Not in revolution. But in the serene confidence of men who believed that reason, properly applied, could make a new humanity.

Their experiments were small.

Their consequences were enormous.

Chapter 8
Freedom Without Excuse

By the late nineteenth century, the revolutionary fervor of the Jacobins had long since burned out. Europe had wearied of moral crusades, of virtue enforced at knife-point, of the impossible attempt to regenerate mankind through terror.

The age of blood gave way to the age of steam. Factories, railways, telegraphs, and engines replaced the rhetoric of virtue with the language of efficiency.

Yet beneath this calm lay a continuation of the Enlightenment project.

The ambition to remake man did not vanish. It changed its instruments.

Where Rousseau had spoken of virtue, and Robespierre of purification, the new age spoke of optimization, scientific management, behavior, systems, inputs and outputs, efficiency, measurement, prediction, and control.

The tone moderated. The goals remained.

For the first time, man was no longer purified, educated, or redeemed. He was managed.

Fredrick Winslow Taylor gave this transformation its first systematic form. In *The Principles of Scientific Management* (1911), he proposed that human labor is a solvable problem.

Find the optimal motion.

Measure it.

Standardize it.

Impose it.

Reward compliance.

Remove discretion.

Work became a science. The worker became an instrument — a component in a system designed by experts.

Taylor did not seek to perfect man morally or politically. He sought to perfect him mechanically. In doing so he was the first to treat the human body as a system of *movements to optimize*.

This introduced a new proposition into modern life:
>Freedom is waste.
>Efficiency is justice.
>Optimization is progress.

The language of virtue yielded to the language of metrics. The individual was no longer shaped by reason or terror; he was disciplined by measurement.

While Taylor dissected the motions of the body, behaviorism dissected the motions of the mind.

In 1913, John B. Watson announced a psychology stripped of introspection:
>Consciousness is unreliable.
>Thought is indistinguishable from behavior.
>Only stimulus and response can be measured.

If Taylor reduced labor to motion, Watson reduced mind to mechanism.

Human beings became:
>predictable,
>conditionable,
>programmable,
>observable,
>measurable,
>adjustable.

B.F. Skinner would later refine this into a closed system:
>Behavior is shaped by environment.
>Environment is designable.
>Therefore behavior is designable.

The Enlightenment's perfectibility was now stripped of metaphysics. The makeable man became a subject of conditioning.

In place of Rousseau's "forced to be free", the new formula emerged:
>"Freedom is irrelevant; behavior is what matters."

This was not oppression. It was presented as scientific benevolence — the belief that with proper incentives, cues, and reinforcements, human beings could be guided into more productive lives.

Before psychology turned fully toward measurement, William James had sensed the direction of travel. In *The Principles of Psychology* (1890), he described the mind as lived, fluid, irreducible. Yet even as the work appeared, the field moved away from that vision. "A nasty little subject; all one cares to know lies outside it", he remarked, as psychology shifted toward reflexes, physiology, and control.[20]

James stands here as the last humanist before the age of optimization — a reminder that psychology once sought to understand the self before it learned to manage it.

The technocrats would soon extend this logic to society as a whole.

They believed the future belonged not to politicians or priests, but to engineers.

And why not?

They had mastered steel.

They had mastered electricity.

They had mastered production.

They had mastered the measurable world.

Why should they not master society itself?

To the technocrat, society is a system.

Systems have inputs. Inputs can be optimized. Optimization produces harmony. Harmony justifies authority. Politics becomes engineering. Citizens become data. Freedom becomes a design parameter.

---

[20] William James's remark appears in the *Biographical Note* preceding *The Principles of Psychology*, in *Great Books of the Western World*, Vol. 53, Encyclopædia Britannica, Chicago, 1952: "After publication of the *Principles*, James lost interest in this 'nasty little subject; all one cares to know lies outside it.'"

This was the quiet revolution — the moment when control replaced coercion, and management replaced morality. No terror. No sermons. No barricades.

Just systems.

FREEDOM WITHOUT EXCUSE

In the Taylorist-technocratic worldview, freedom becomes something subtle — almost invisible.

It is no longer a metaphysical right, nor an ethical obligation, nor the capacity to judge one's own good. It becomes a performance variable — tolerated only insofar as it does not interfere with optimization.

Man is no longer purified or perfected. He is rendered efficient.

He is no longer a sinner or a citizen. He is a component.

The Enlightenment had asked, "What might man become?" The technocratic answer was simpler — and more dangerous, "Whatever the system requires."

Until the modern age, freedom was always understood in relation to some external moral structure — the cosmos, the law, the Church, the virtues, natural right, or inherited custom. Man lived within an order, not apart from it. Freedom was constrained where it conflicted with that order, yet its existence was excused and justified by the very frameworks that limited it. Submission could be enforced, doctrine imposed, individuals indoctrinated — but no society imagined that the human impulse toward freedom, the internal architecture of desire and will, could be removed. The structures above man assumed that the drive for freedom was built into man.

Freedom had an excuse.

The technocratic society abandons this view. It treats freedom not as a moral category, but as a behavioral variable — something to be shaped, redirected, or overwritten.

Freedom survives only where it does not interfere.

When it does, it is not punished. It is not excused as something to be overcome. It is adjusted.

This is freedom without excuse.

Earlier societies shaped behavior from the outside — through sermons, punishments, rituals, and social pressure. They governed conduct, but did not presume they could redesign the individual.

Technocracy crosses that line. It no longer *governs* behavior. It *produces it*.

What earlier ages enforced from without, the modern system engineers from within.

Pre-modern manipulation was moral and coercive. Technocratic manipulation is mechanical and predictive.

It appeals not to duty or reverence, but to data, incentives, and design.

For the first time, the system declares:

"We do not merely expect conformity — we can produce it."

The old world governed behavior. The new world engineers preference.

The earlier order punished nonconformity. The technocratic order prevents it. Not by force, but by shaping the conditions under which choice is made.

Freedom ceases to be a right with justification.
It becomes a permission without one.

A new kind of human emerges:
> not virtuous,
> not perfected,
> not regenerated,
> but optimized for the system.

And once optimization becomes the standard, the next step becomes inevitable:
> Design the human being who fits the system.

This is the bridge to the modern age.
The Terror used the guillotine.
The technocrats used the stopwatch.
The future would use the algorithm.

Chapter 9
The Biology of Improvement

The nineteenth century did more than expand the frontiers of science; it altered the boundaries of what people believed could be changed. Where earlier ages sought to improve mankind through instruction, virtue, and political reform, the modern age entertained a more radical possibility: that the human being himself might be made better at the root.

Biology, newly confident after Darwin, seemed to reveal a mechanism beneath the mysteries of heredity — a mechanism that could be guided, corrected, and improved.

This idea did not begin in darkness. It arose from the century's most characteristic virtues: faith in progress, the humanitarian impulse to relieve suffering, and the conviction that knowledge, properly applied, could overcome the accidents of nature. If disease could be prevented, if sanitation could rescue cities, if vaccination could conquer pestilence, why should society accept the arbitrary distribution of inherited afflictions? Why should the future be hostage to the past?

Yet embedded in this benevolence was a new assumption: that human nature was not simply lived, but selectable; not only received, but improvable; not merely shaped by society, but available to a deeper kind of design.

Eugenics was the first modern attempt to treat the human being as biological material — material that could be measured, ranked, encouraged, or withheld. It was a project born not of cruelty but of confidence, and that confidence would become the foundation for later efforts to reengineer man by political, ideological, and technological means.

What began as biology would soon become a template.

Before the nineteenth century, schemes to improve mankind worked with ideas, customs, virtues, and political arrangements. The human being himself — his temperament, abilities, and character — was taken as given. If he failed, it was because he had succumbed to vice, ignorance, poor governance, or moral disorder. Remedy lay in instruction, example, or discipline. The forge hammered the world around man; it did not claim to hammer the man himself.

The nineteenth century altered that horizon. Emerging from the scientific revolution and carried by the prestige of the Enlightenment, biology announced a new possibility: perhaps human nature was not fixed at all, but open to improvement by design.

If so, the ancient boundary between the given and the made — between inheritance and intention — could be crossed not only in politics, but in the structure of the human organism itself.

This was the genesis of eugenics — confidence mistaken for compassion.

Behaviorism would later shape conduct through habit; eugenics moved upstream, treating biology itself as the site of correction.

Heredity, newly illuminated after Darwin, seemed neither mystical nor opaque. It was a mechanism, and all mechanisms suggest the possibility of refinement. If nature, left alone, distributed intelligence, vigor, and health unevenly, why should society accept these distributions as destiny? If the calamities that haunted human life — disease, deformity, hereditary illness — could be reduced or prevented, was it not an act of justice to do so?

The argument acquired moral force precisely because it borrowed the language of beneficence rather than domination. To many in the nineteenth century, eugenics appeared not as tyranny but as mercy — an extension of the humanitarian project equipped with the tools of modern science.

Where earlier ages prayed for deliverance from misfortune, this age believed it had found the method.

Yet beneath this aspiration lay a decisive shift.

Here for the first time in Western thought, the human being himself became material — not metaphorically, not spiritually, but biologically available to improvement. The question was no longer how a man should live, but what sort of man should exist.

Darwin had described *natural* selection. Others now sought to impose *directed* selection upon man.

Whether applied gently or severely, publicly or privately, through incentives or coercion, the underlying assumption remained:

> Human nature is not a boundary.
> It is a blueprint.

From this conviction flowed the first great biological program of modernity — and with it, the belief that man could be shaped at the root, not the branch.

Eugenics treated the human being not as a problem to be mitigated, but one to be solved.

GALTON AND THE STATISTICAL HUMAN

Eugenics begins with a single intuition, and that intuition belonged to Francis Galton, Charles Darwin's younger cousin. Darwin had explained how species change across time; Galton asked whether mankind might accelerate the process. If evolution operated without foresight, could human intelligence provide the foresight evolution lacked?

Where nature was slow, wasteful, and indifferent, might society be made swift, economical, and directed?

Underlying these questions was a deeper transformation in knowledge itself. Earlier generations studied individuals; Galton studied populations. He sought not the exceptional man, but the average one — the statistical center around which variation clustered.

Once variation could be plotted, tabulated, sorted, and ranked, it seemed to acquire impersonal law. What had once belonged to providence or fortune now appeared as a distribution.

From this, Galton drew his conclusion:

If traits are heritable,

and if traits are unevenly distributed,

then improvement requires improving heredity itself.

He believed this not in the spirit of oppression, but of civic duty. His work carries the optimism of Victorian science — faith in measurement, classification, and steady improvement.

He proposed encouragement for the "fit", discouragement for the "unfit", and public recognition for hereditary merit. In his hands, eugenics was not yet state machinery; it was a program of stewardship.

But the heart of his project was measurement.

Once the qualities of the mind could be quantified — reaction time, perception, cognition — society would possess the means to distinguish, rank, and intervene.

A new human being appeared: not the soul of theology, nor the citizen of political theory, but the statistical human — a point within a distribution.

This was the decisive step.

For once man is conceived *statistically*, intervention moves from the individual to the population. Problems once addressed by charity or reform become problems of adjustment at scale.

If variation is measurable, improvement appears calculable. If improvement is calculable, it appears administrable.

Galton supplied the framework. Others would supply the power.

THE HUMANITARIAN TURN

To modern readers, eugenics appears self-evidently sinister.

It did not appear so to its earliest advocates.

In the late nineteenth and early twentieth centuries, it attracted reformers, physicians, clergy, and social progressives. They embraced it not as cruelty, but as remedy.

The industrial age had revealed entire classes burdened by illness, disability, and poverty. If these conditions were hereditary, then no amount of charity could erase them.

The humanitarian project faced a choice:

Accept the permanence of suffering,

or attempt to prevent its transmission.

Eugenics offered the second.

It promised fewer children born into affliction, fewer families burdened by inherited disease, fewer lives constrained by conditions beyond effort.

It spoke the language of "better babies", "fitter families", and "public health". It seemed to extend the same logic that had conquered disease.

At first, it was not coercive. Its advocates preferred education, incentives, voluntary participation, and public encouragement of what they called "responsible parenthood". They saw themselves as custodians of welfare, not engineers of destiny. In their view, the burden of inherited illness fell not only upon families but upon the wider society — hospitals, asylums, prisons, and charitable institutions. Eugenics appeared not as domination but as sanitary reform, the biological counterpart to clean water, vaccination, and urban planning.

Yet a structural flaw was already present.

Once society accepts that some lives are more desirable than others, the line between guidance and control begins to dissolve.

What begins as encouragement becomes pressure. What begins as advice becomes policy. And once the state defines hereditary value, the freedom to exist as one is begins to erode.

The Progressive embrace of eugenics was not a deviation from the spirit of the age. It was its expression.

The next step followed naturally.

WHEN THE STATE TAKES HOLD

Eugenics began as enthusiasm. It did not remain so.

Once heredity became a public concern, governments confronted a new question: if hereditary defects burden society, does society not have the right — perhaps the obligation — to reduce those burdens?

What charity could not prevent, what education could not remedy, what institutions could only manage, the state now sought to eliminate.

The shift was subtle, but decisive.

Reformers argued that hereditary illness and disability imposed costs on the public treasury and suffering upon families already overburdened. Physicians argued that diseases long considered fate were in fact forms of inherited degeneration. Legislators argued that preventing future misery was an act of compassion. Judges argued that the state already constrained liberty for the sake of public safety; why should inherited suffering be exempt?

Within this framework, coercion appeared consistent.

By the early twentieth century, sterilization laws appeared across the United States and Europe. Those deemed "unfit" were prevented from reproducing as institutionalization acquired this new function. Marriage restrictions and immigration controls completed the architecture.

Private organizations also participated in the eugenic project. Margaret Sanger, founder of what would later become Planned Parenthood, spoke of birth control as a means of preventing the reproduction of those she termed the "unfit." She favored voluntary methods rather than state coercion, yet her language reflected the broader conviction of the age: that heredity could be managed for the public good. Her movement overlapped with eugenic societies, shared conferences, and adopted much of the same vocabulary.

Birth control advocacy, though often voluntary in method, shared the language of hereditary management. These measures also were justified through the language of public health. Disease had been conquered by sanitation, pestilence by quarantine, infection by vaccination — why should hereditary affliction not be handled with equal scientific decisiveness? Many of the same reformers who championed clean water and food safety now championed eugenics. To them the continuity was moral, not tyrannical.

The tragedy lies not in intention, but in logic.

For once the state assumes the authority to judge which hereditary traits are worthy of reproduction, the value of the individual subtly shifts. He ceases to be a moral being possessed of inherent dignity; he becomes a carrier of traits, a bearer of genetic assets or liabilities.

Human value becomes an actuarial calculation.

THE TRAGEDY OF REDUCTION

Eugenics rests on a reduction: that human nature can be understood and improved through heredity alone.

This reduction was not malicious. It reflected the scientific spirit of the age — its confidence in mechanism and progress, its belief in progress, and its enthusiasm for the application of knowledge to the relief of suffering.

But heredity, isolated, becomes distortion.

Human beings are influenced by inheritance, but not defined by it. The qualities that define a life — courage, judgment, loyalty, imagination — do not follow simple curves.

By reducing man to heredity, eugenics mistook variation for defect and potential for destiny.

It treated complexity as noise. Individuality as deviation. Chance as error.

The tragedy is not merely that coercion followed.

It is that the vision of man was diminished.

Human life ceased to be inheritance.

It became a material

THE LEGACY

Though eugenics declined after the Second World War, its logic did not disappear.

It migrated.

From biology to ideology.

From heredity to history.

From physical traits to social ones.

The premise remained: human nature is makeable.

Marxist regimes would attempt to create the "new man" through ideology. Purges removed those deemed incompatible. Conditioning reshaped those who remained.

Maoism extended this into thought itself.

Even democratic societies absorbed the impulse — through social science, policy, and behavioral design.

The instruments changed.

The logic did not.

Eugenics revealed a new way of thinking about mankind: as a variable in a system, a subject for improvement, an object for design.

Where earlier ages accepted limits, the modern age questioned them.

Where earlier ages governed behavior, the modern age sought to redesign the person beneath it.

This chapter began with heredity. It ends with something larger. Once man is considered makeable, no obvious boundary remains.

The next chapters will follow this movement — from body to belief, from biology to ideology.

The forge has shifted. From nature to history.

Chapter 10
The Bolshevik Project
– Engineering the New Soviet Man

The Bolshevik Revolution was not merely a seizure of power. It was an attempt to reconfigure the human being through the reconfiguration of society. Marx had argued that man was shaped by his material conditions; Lenin transformed this observation into a governing program. If consciousness was determined by the world, then a new world — purified of class, hierarchy, and exploitation — might shape a new consciousness in turn.

In this sense, Bolshevism did not introduce a novel anthropology so much as consolidate several that had preceded it. Enlightenment rationalism, Rousseauian moral plasticity, Jacobin coercion, technocratic administration, demographic calculation, and early biological optimization converged into a single political project.

The revolution was not simply political.
It was anthropological.

Where eugenics had sought to improve the human stock through biology, the Bolsheviks sought to improve the human being through history. They believed that the entire structure of society — its classes, loyalties, habits, institutions, and inherited identities — could be dissolved and rebuilt according to a scientific plan.

The past was not a guide. It was raw material.

What eugenicists had expected from heredity, the Bolsheviks expected from revolution: that the forge would yield a better human type.

Lenin viewed destruction as a creative act. Class enemies were not individuals but categories; they could be removed as a class, and society would be improved in the process. The Party became the engineer, the state the instrument, and history the laboratory.

The goal was nothing less than the manufacture of a new kind of man — disciplined, collectivist, selfless, ideologically pure, and freed from the alienation of bourgeois life.

LENIN WEAPONIZES MARX

Marx had described the movement of history; Lenin sought to direct it. He believed that revolution needed not merely to occur but to be made.

Marx had spoken of the proletariat becoming conscious of its condition. Lenin concluded that the proletariat would never reach such consciousness on its own. It must be awakened — and led — by a disciplined vanguard.

This vanguard, the Communist Party, was not a political organization in the ordinary sense. It was an instrument of historical necessity — a mechanism through which revolution could be accelerated, directed, and secured.

Lenin believed that history had a destination. The Party's task was to force the path toward it.

If backwardness, superstition, private interest, or inherited attachments slowed the advance, they were obstacles to be cleared.

Destruction became part of the method.

Revolutionary thought had long suggested that crisis could serve as a catalyst. Even John Adams had once written, "the worse, the better",[21] meaning that only extremity could rouse a

---

[21] John Adams to Elbridge Gerry, July 4, 1814: "Five and forty years ago... my invariable answer was, 'The worse, the better.' Nothing ever did arouse this People, but the last and extremest expression and exertion of the Contempt, the malice and vengeance of Great Britain, and thus in my opinion We shall soon see and feel."

passive nation. By the early twentieth century, Lenin's faction embraced the principle openly:

Collapse was not danger; it was precondition.

In Lenin's hands, Marxism ceased to be a critique of society and became an engine for remaking it. Social wreckage was not to be feared; it was to be used. In Lenin's hands, Marxism ceased to be a critique of society and became an engine for remaking it.

The making of a new world implied the making of a new man.

CLASS AS A HEREDITARY ANALOGUE

Earlier class systems sorted individuals *within* society. Lenin's system sorted society in order to determine who must be *removed* from it.

Class became not a position, but a verdict. The old hierarchies had been the fabric of social order; the Bolshevik hierarchy was a system of targets. Class became not a position in society but a verdict upon the person identifying what the revolution must destroy.

These classifications functioned like hereditary traits. One might renounce belief, adopt new loyalties, or labor with zeal, but one could not escape class identity. It adhered like a genetic marker.

The kulak was not merely a farmer of means.
He was a bearer of a social essence.

The bourgeois was not merely a man with property.
He was a carrier of bourgeois consciousness.

Thus the revolution's first great act of engineering was purification.

Categories deemed incompatible with the future were not to be reformed.
They were to be removed.

Purging a class was presented not as cruelty, but as hygiene.

This was ideological eugenics — the elimination of human types defined not by biology, but by social origin.

PURGE, THEN TERROR

The Stalinist period made explicit what had been implicit from the beginning. Between collectivization, famine, executions, and the Gulag system, millions perished — not as individuals judged by deed, but as categories judged by definition.

The purge came first. Terror followed. Only after the human landscape had been cleared did terror become the means of shaping those who remained.

Fear was not incidental to the system; it *was* the system. Terror functioned as a form of behavioral conditioning. Arrests occurred without warning. Releases proved temporary. Confessions were extracted through psychological and physical pressure. Friends informed on friends, neighbors on neighbors, colleagues on colleagues. Loyalty was measured not through conviction but through the avoidance of suspicion.

Society learned hesitation — the reflex that terror requires. The boundary between safety and danger became invisible, and because it was invisible, uncertainty was omnipresent. The result was a population trained to conform, not by persuasion, and not even by force, but by the unpredictability of when force might fall.

This was the second phase of ideological eugenics: not the elimination of incompatible types, but the shaping of a compliant remainder.

SOCIETY AS LABORATORY

Once resistance had been removed or subdued, the state turned to construction.

The Soviet Union[22] became a laboratory for the production of the New Soviet Man.

The family was reorganized; schools became factories of political education; workplaces became instruments of social discipline; private life dissolved into the communal; religious practices, and inherited loyalties were discouraged or forbidden.

The aim was to produce a population whose instincts aligned with the needs of the collective. Virtue was no longer a matter of personal character but of political conformity. Sincerity was measured by enthusiasm in public rituals and denunciations. Private thought became suspect; only ideological transparency was safe.

The new society was meant to produce a new human being — one in whom individuality had been subordinated to the arc of history. The system did not ask the individual to believe. It asked him to become.

Where eugenics trusted biology, the Bolsheviks trusted environment.

Man would be shaped by the world that surrounded him.

Consciousness would be cast in the mold of the system.

THE FAILURE OF THE EXPERIMENT

The project failed for reasons rooted in the very nature it sought to overcome. Fear can enforce obedience. It cannot generate conviction.

---

[22] "Soviet" (совет) originally meant *council* — a local assembly of workers, soldiers, or peasants formed during the Russian revolutions of 1905 and 1917. These soviets were not uniform bodies but often competing, chaotic, and locally autonomous organs claiming to represent "the people" against the old order. After the Bolshevik seizure of power, the hundreds of major soviets, and well over a thousand local ones, were progressively centralized, subordinated to party control, and fused into the structure of the new state — the Union of Soviet Socialist Republics (USSR), literally a "union of councils," though the councils themselves soon lost independence.

Bureaucracy can administer society. It cannot produce virtue. Ideology can command public enthusiasm. It cannot compel private belief. The New Soviet Man proved elusive because human beings interpret, resist, adapt, and endure in ways no system can fully predict. Corruption flourished. Cynicism replaced sincerity. Parallel lives emerged — one public, one private. The revolution sought transparency. It produced division.

The experiment revealed the limit of historical engineering: society can be reorganized, but the depth of human character resists design.

LEGACY

The Bolshevik project was the first great attempt to engineer man through history. Its tools were not genes, but classes; not heredity, but consciousness; not biology, but ideology. It demonstrated how easily the shaping of society becomes the shaping of the human being himself.

Over its seventy-four years, the Soviet system consumed between fifteen and twenty million lives through executions, deportations, forced collectivization, and engineered famine. More than eighteen million people passed through the Gulags.

Yet the deeper lesson is not numerical. It is structural. Its reach was vast; its imprint enduring.

An engineered anthropology can take hold quickly. Its consequences recede slowly.

The next chapter carries this logic further — into Maoism, where the remaking of consciousness becomes explicit and continuous, and where the transformation of the self is no longer a byproduct of revolution, but its primary aim.

Chapter 11
Maoism and Perpetual Purification

If Bolshevism sought to engineer man through the apparatus of history, Maoism sought to do so through the perpetual purification of consciousness.

Lenin believed destruction was a creative act.

Mao believed it must never stop. Revolution, in his hands, was not an event but a condition — a force to be renewed, intensified, and reapplied to the human being without end.

Mao's China followed a different temporal path than the Soviet Union. The first revolutionary order, established in 1949, nearly destroyed itself during the Great Leap Forward and the Cultural Revolution. After Mao's death in 1976, the Party carried out a second founding — a reinvention under Deng Xiaoping that preserved political control while discarding much of Maoist practice.

In this sense, the Chinese Communist Party (CCP) reset its own clock, prolonging the life of a system that had already exhausted one revolutionary cycle.

The People's Republic began with a premise more demanding than loyalty: the inner life itself must align with the Party's truth. Where Soviet rule divided the population into categories of trust and suspicion, Maoism dissolved the categories entirely.

Everyone was a potential revolutionary. Everyone was a potential enemy. The distinction depended on thought — and thought was material to be reshaped.

The Cultural Revolution carried this logic to its highest expression. China did not merely reorganize society. It sought to remake the soul.

THE LOGIC OF PERPETUAL REVOLUTION

Mao believed revolutions decay. Victory produces complacency; institutions harden; elites detach from the masses; memory pulls society back toward what it has been. The greatest threat was not the enemy outside. It was stagnation within. To preserve revolution, society must be kept in motion.

"Revolution is not a dinner party," Mao declared — not an orderly or polite affair, but a struggle against the past embedded in the living. [23] Class enemies were not confined to groups. They lived in habits, customs, traditions, language, buildings, and memory itself. Revolution therefore required purification without end. Every element of life could be examined, criticized, denounced, and rebuilt. The aim was not stability. It was controlled instability — a society suspended between what it had been and what it was commanded to become.

THE DESTRUCTION OF THE FOUR OLDS

The Cultural Revolution began as an assault on memory. Mao called for the elimination of the Four Olds:
old ideas,
old culture,
old customs,
old habits.

---

[23] The phrase "Revolution is not a dinner party" appears in Mao Zedong's *Report on an Investigation of the Peasant Movement in Hunan* (1927), commonly called the Hunan Report. Written after several months observing peasant uprisings in Hunan Province, the Report endorsed the spontaneous violence of the rural poor, argued that revolution required "class struggle with a vengeance", and insisted that the peasantry — not the urban proletariat — would be the primary engine of Chinese revolution. Its analysis and rhetoric shaped the Party's land reform campaigns in the 1930s and 1940s and later furnished ideological justification for the Cultural Revolution.
The Report later inspired radical movements from the Naxalites in India to the Shining Path in Peru, each seeking to reproduce Mao's model of revolutionary purification.

It was not enough to remove political opponents or reorganize the economy. The symbolic world itself had to be broken — temples, ancestral tablets, classical texts, religious practices, family hierarchies, Confucian virtues. All inherited forms of meaning was declared an obstacle to the revolutionary future.

Red Guards became the instruments of this destruction. They tore down relics, burned books, renamed streets, humiliated teachers, and forced public renunciations. The aim was not vandalism. It was anthropological. Continuity was the enemy. Roots were the enemy. The Cultural Revolution attacked not only belief, but the frameworks in which belief could exist.

Where eugenics had sought to improve the human stock by altering heredity, Maoism sought to improve the human type by erasing cultural memory.

THOUGHT REFORM

Long before the Cultural Revolution, Maoism had pioneered a method more radical than Soviet indoctrination. Compliance was not enough. Agreement was not enough. The revolution had to be experienced inwardly.

Thought reform operated through three instruments:
> Confession, which stripped away the inherited self and forced individuals to articulate their faults in public.
> Criticism, in which friends, colleagues, and neighbors exposed one another's ideological impurities.
> Struggle, in which the self was dissolved and rebuilt through sustained collective pressure.

Where Bolshevism shaped behavior, Maoism sought to reshape the inner life. The goal was psychological transparency. A person must not only act correctly. He must think correctly. And thinking correctly meant thinking as the Party thought.

This produced a new anthropology:
> A human being whose interior world was not private but collective,
>
> not protected but exposed,
>
> not stable but malleable.

The revolution aimed to produce a soul without shadow.

ENGINEERED LOYALTY

Under Maoism, loyalty was not a state. It was a performance. It had to be demonstrated continuously — through slogans, denunciations, rituals, marches, and visible enthusiasm. To fail to display loyalty was to invite suspicion. Suspicion became a verdict.

Fear became pedagogy. A careless remark, an old photograph, an insufficient applause — any could become evidence. Loyalty was not expected. It was engineered through the constant pressure to reaffirm allegiance.

People learned to monitor themselves. Children corrected parents. Students overthrew teachers. Groups competed in displays of purity.

Sincerity collapsed into performance. Performance hardened into habit.

SOCIETY AS A LANDSCAPE OF TARGETS

As the Cultural Revolution expanded, the targets multiplied. Faction fought faction; Red Guards fought Red Guards; armies fought armies; ministries collapsed; families fractured; institutions dissolved.

Purification became a moving target. No one could be certain who the next enemy was, because the enemy was a shifting function of the revolutionary will. Identity became fluid, not by liberation but by danger. Safety could not be found in conformity, because conformity itself was redefined at every moment.

In Mao's China, the revolution devoured its own children not by accident but by logic. A system that requires perpetual purification perpetually betrays the premise it stands on. Each new stage of the revolution required a new impurity to destroy.

This was autocracy in its most radical form: the engineered instability of an entire civilization.

THE FAILURE OF PERPETUAL PURIFICATION

The Cultural Revolution ended through exhaustion. Human beings can endure fear. They cannot endure endless transformation. The attempt to dissolve and rebuild the inner life produced not purity, but fatigue; not loyalty, but resignation.

As in the Soviet Union, cynicism replaced sincerity and the double life became universal. People spoke in the language of the revolution but lived in its shadow, maintaining the forms of ideological purity while privately retreating into silence.

The system reshaped not only behavior, but the inner architecture of the self. What could not be spoken aloud was carried inward. The revolution sought a transparent soul. It produced a divided one, echoing the Soviet result.

The failure was not accidental. Human nature resists infinite remaking. A self can be pressured, reshaped, even broken. It cannot be rebuilt without end.

LEGACY

Maoism represents the most extreme expression of the modern radical urge — the belief that man can be remade continually, not once or twice, but indefinitely. It showed that the impulse to engineer humanity does not stop at society's edge; it reaches inward, toward the self, demanding that identity become a permanent construction site. The CCP that arose from

China's revolutionary upheavals has now endured for more than seventy years, though in a form reshaped after 1978, when the Party reinvented itself following the Cultural Revolution. Across its revolutionary arc, China lost between thirty and forty-five million people in the Great Leap Forward and another one to two million during the Cultural Revolution, with tens of millions more subjected to struggle sessions, denunciations, and the laogai labor system.[24] This second founding reset the regime's historical clock, allowing a system damaged by perpetual purification to persist through new methods rather than new ideals. [25]

The Bolshevik project had sought to engineer man through the apparatus of history. Maoism sought to engineer him through perpetual purification. Both revealed the same underlying transformation: once human nature is considered makeable, there is no obvious boundary at which the project must stop.

The next stage will follow that transformation into the democratic world, where the engineering impulse has not disappeared but changed its character. The tools are different, the methods subtler, the instruments quieter — yet the presumption remains the same: that human behavior can be shaped, managed, guided, and designed.

---

[24] Struggle sessions were public rituals of accusation and forced confession during which individuals were denounced, humiliated, and compelled to admit ideological error before a crowd, often under coercion or violence. The laogai ("reform through labor") system consisted of a vast network of forced labor camps used to imprison, reeducate, and exploit those deemed politically or socially deviant. Both functioned not merely as instruments of punishment, but as mechanisms for reshaping thought and enforcing ideological conformity.

[25] If one treats the post-1978 reforms as a second institutional founding rather than a continuation of Maoist revolutionary governance, the contemporary Chinese Communist Party would reach the Soviet Union's seventy-four-year lifespan in 2052. This observation is chronological, not predictive, but interesting nonetheless.

Part IV:
The Therapeutic Turn
(1950 – Present)

Chapter 12
Behaviorism, Childhood, and the Scientific Family

Behaviorism promised a science of prediction, and postwar America welcomed it. John Watson declared that with the right environment he could shape any infant into any kind of adult. B. F. Skinner built a system in which behavior could be conditioned, reinforced, and optimized. Benjamin Spock translated these impulses into mass culture, turning parenting into a domain governed by expertise, manuals, and measured outcomes.

For the first time in modern history, the home — not only the school, factory, or state — became a site of deliberate engineering. The child was no longer simply raised. The child was *shaped*. The family became therapeutic, managerial, and scientific.

This chapter follows the migration of the engineering ambition into private life — where it appears not as tyranny, but as guidance; not as coercion, but as care — the gentle machinery of the therapeutic age.

THE SCIENTIFIC FAMILY

By the mid-twentieth century, a new arena stood ready for engineering: the home.

Unlike Bolshevik or Maoist systems, democratic societies did not mobilize armies or reorganize class structures. They turned to expertise. The promise was gentler — and therefore more persuasive: if children could be understood scientifically, they could be raised more wisely; if parents followed proper method, development itself might become reliable, predictable, and improvable.

Parenthood, once governed by custom and inheritance, increasingly deferred to psychological authority. Advice columns, pediatric manuals, government pamphlets, radio, and television carried the same message: the child is not merely born; the child is made. Not by revolution. By technique.

MODERN PSYCHOLOGY COMES HOME

Freud had made childhood decisive for the fate of the adult. Behaviorism extended the claim: childhood was not only decisive — it was *programmable.*

For Watson, the infant was not a mystery of temperament but an input system awaiting conditioning. "Give me a dozen healthy infants," he declared, and he could train any one of them "to become any type of specialist" he might select. [26] The statement was boastful, reckless, and rhetorically loaded — yet its underlying confidence shaped the century that followed.

If heredity could be bypassed, and if the mind could be molded by stimulus and reinforcement, then the family became the primary apparatus of social engineering. What the state attempted on populations, parents were now encouraged to attempt — calmly — on children.

The home became a workshop of developmental outcomes.

THE RISE OF PARENTING BY BLUEPRINT

American behavioral psychology and mid-century consumer culture reinforced one another.

---

[26] John B. Watson, "Psychology as the Behaviorist Views It" (1913), and later popularized in *Behaviorism* (1924). Watson's claim — that environment could override heredity — became one of the most quoted statements in twentieth-century psychology.

The message was simple: correct method produces correct results. Spock softened Watson's severity, replacing detachment with affection, yet retained the central assumption: the child's nature is modifiable, and expert knowledge can guide that modification. [27] Postwar optimism and rising affluence created the ideal setting. Every aspect of childhood — sleep, feeding, discipline, praise, autonomy — could be optimized.

Parents were encouraged to observe as technicians observe systems: identify maladaptive inputs, correct dysfunctional routines, optimize the behavioral environment. Love remained essential. But increasingly, it functioned within a system.

A new anthropology entered the nursery: the child as project.

BEHAVIORISM: THOUGHT REDUCED TO OUTPUT

Behaviorism's appeal lay not in philosophical depth, but in *operational clarity*. It treated the mind as a black box: internal states could be ignored so long as inputs and outputs were measurable.

What mattered was what a child *did*, not what a child *was*. Behavior became controllable. Misbehavior became correctable. Personality became a trajectory shaped by reward schedules.

Skinner refined this into a system:
> Behavior is shaped by environment.
> Environment is designable.
> Therefore behavior is designable.

Where Watson asserted, Skinner calibrated. His devices, reinforcement schedules, and programmed learning expressed a single conviction: freedom is noise, structure is signal. [28] If

---

[27] Benjamin Spock's *The Common Sense Book of Baby and Child Care* (1946) became one of the best-selling books of the twentieth century. While rejecting Watson's rigidity, it preserved the assumption that child-rearing should follow scientifically informed guidance.

[28] B. F. Skinner developed teaching machines and programmed instruction in the 1950s, notably in *Science and Human Behavior* (1953). His work shaped mid-century educational reform and cemented behaviorism's influence beyond the laboratory.

behavior could be shaped precisely, the self could be shaped indirectly.

CHILDHOOD AS A CONTROLLED ENVIRONMENT

By the late 1950s and early 1960s, childhood had methodically become the central institution through which liberal democracies pursued social reform. The expansion of compulsory education, school counseling, pediatric psychology, and public-health programs created a coordinated model of expert supervision, grounding development not in inherited custom but in scientifically managed environments. [29]

Racial desegregation, educational equity, new expectations for gender, therapeutic understandings of emotion, and concerns about delinquency all converged on the same object: *the developing child.*

If the child could be shaped, the future could be guided.
If the family could be guided, society could be stabilized.

Schools became laboratories of socialization; pediatric offices became advisory centers; television programming became instructional habitat. The expansion of compulsory education completed the system. Childhood was now not merely a stage of life but a managed environment, a zone where expertise replaced custom.[30]

---

[29] The transformation of childhood into a primary vehicle for social reform is well documented in mid-century policy literature. Works such as Urie Bronfenbrenner's *Two Worlds of Childhood* (1970), the emergence of child-guidance clinics beginning in the 1920s, and federal initiatives like the 1965 Head Start program placed developmental science at the center of public welfare strategy.

[30] By the 1950s, school psychology had become one of the fastest-growing applied fields. The National Defense Education Act (1958) funded testing and counseling programs; Carl Rogers's client-centered therapy influenced guidance curricula; and Benjamin Bloom's *Taxonomy of Educational Objectives* (1956) reframed schooling around measurable behavioral outcomes.

Childhood ceased to be a stage. It became a system. The goal was humane. But beneath the ideal lay a familiar assumption: the child is material.

THE CULTURAL CONSEQUENCE

Scientific parenting did not produce the utopian consistency it promised. Children remained unpredictable, willful, imaginative, resistant. Parents oscillated between confidence and anxiety. Professional advice remained certain even as contradictory recommendations proliferated, and families found themselves in a new kind of unease: not ignorance, but over-instruction.

The deeper transformation was subtler. Parenthood ceased to be inheritance. It became competency. Love remained essential. Expertise became authoritative. The authority of the family receded as the authority of psychology advanced.

The child, once formed by kinship and tradition, was increasingly shaped by designed developmental pathways. The family remained the vessel, but Science increasingly claimed the helm.

LEGACY

Behaviorism and the scientific family did not produce a fully designed child. Nor did they collapse into coercion. Instead, they reshaped the democratic imagination through seemingly unobtrusive means, yet pursuing ambitions no less transformative than the great revolutions that came before.

They taught societies to think of development as an engineering problem:

    If behavior is unhealthy, adjust the environment.
    If emotion is maladaptive, modify the stimulus.
    If outcomes diverge, redesign the inputs.

Where revolutionary regimes sought to reshape man through force, democratic societies sought to reshape him through guidance. The tools differed profoundly. The presumption did not: human nature is adjustable, human behavior is improvable by design.

The next chapter follows this presumption into public life — the rise of the therapeutic state, where governance justifies itself not by divine right or historical destiny, but by its promise to diagnose, treat, and improve the human condition.

Chapter 13
The Therapeutic State

By the mid-twentieth century, democratic societies faced a paradox. They had rejected the coercive engineering of the totalitarian states — no purges, no thought police, no cultural revolutions — and yet they confronted social problems that appeared resistant to law alone. Poverty, crime, addiction, delinquency, inequality, unrest: these were no longer interpreted chiefly as failures of order or morality. Increasingly, they were framed as failures of adjustment, maladaptations, or unhealthy environments.

A new question emerged in the democratic world: What if social problems were psychological problems?

Once that question entered public policy, the logic of governance shifted. The citizen — once defined by duties, rights, and participation — was recast as a developing being whose emotions, attitudes, and internal states could be improved through guidance. Public institutions absorbed the therapeutic vocabulary of psychology, and the result was a new form of statecraft: **rule by interpretation, intervention, and advice**.

The premise was benign; the transformation was profound.

FROM THE CITIZEN TO THE PSYCHOLOGICAL SUBJECT

The expansion of public schooling, child-development science, workplace psychology, and family counseling had prepared the way. But after the Second World War, especially from the 1950s through the 1970s, governments increasingly adopted a therapeutic framework for understanding the individual. Courts spoke of rehabilitation rather than punishment. Schools spoke of self-esteem rather than discipline.

Welfare programs emphasized emotional support alongside financial aid. Employers were encouraged to provide morale training and group sessions. Television and mass media became vehicles for social messaging, often framed in the language of well-being and adjustment.

A new political anthropology was taking shape. The citizen was becoming a **psychological subject** — someone governed not only by law but by therapeutic expectation.

Where earlier political theory assumed an adult moral agent, the therapeutic state[31] increasingly assumed a fragile, developing, emotionally vulnerable being whose flourishing required expert management. Human nature itself became something to be stewarded.

POLICY AS THERAPY

By the 1960s and 1970s, entire sectors of governance were reorganized around therapeutic rationales. Schools became laboratories of emotional development, equipped with counselors, diagnostics, and behavioral interventions. Courts experimented with diversion programs, social workers, and therapeutic jurisprudence. Social services framed dependency, addiction, and unemployment as psychological struggles requiring treatment. Public health campaigns targeted everything from seat belts to sexuality with messaging rooted in behavioral modification. Media institutions framed civic issues — racism, sexism, nuclear fear, the Cold War — in terms of fear, trauma, anxiety, and wellness.

The goal was not punishment or purgation. It was adjustment, guidance, support, prevention, and intervention. This was social engineering without its revolutionary clothing —

---

[31] The phrase "therapeutic state" is associated with sociologist Philip Rieff and later elaborated by Christopher Lasch and Thomas Szasz. It refers to a form of governance in which psychological categories, rather than moral or civic ones, supply the rationale for administrative action.

a redesign of behavior through inputs, environments, and nudges rather than commands.

What began in laboratories and clinics became administrative routine. A new principle entered government:

> If an outcome is undesirable, adjust the environment.
> If the environment cannot be adjusted, adjust the person.

Policy became therapy, and the population became a patient.

THE RISE OF PSYCHOLOGICAL CITIZENSHIP

As psychology expanded, so did its categories.

Normality and abnormality shifted from moral terms to diagnostic ones. Identity, once primarily civic or familial, increasingly took on therapeutic meaning — one's history of wounds, one's childhood environment, one's emotional needs.

Citizenship became tangled with self-esteem, trauma and micro-trauma, psychological safety, developmental support, emotional validation, identity protection

Political movements reshaped themselves accordingly. Arguments formerly grounded in rights or duties now invoked harm, healing, well-being, and psychological threat. Campaigns centered on emotional experience: feeling seen, feeling heard, feeling safe. A new form of legitimacy emerged. Policies were justified not because they were just, but because they were therapeutic. And with that shift, emotion acquired political authority.

SAFETY, TRAUMA, AND THE ADMINISTRATIVE SELF

The therapeutic state introduced a new administrative ideal: the safe society.

Safety once meant physical security from violence. Now it expanded to include psychological security from discomfort, offense, exclusion, instability, and fear.

This shift widened the scope of governance:

> If a workplace caused chronic stress, intervene.
>
> If a school produced feelings of inadequacy, restructure.
>
> If cultural messages triggered anxiety, regulate.
>
> If social conditions generated trauma, redesign them.

The category of "trauma," once reserved for extreme events, expanded into a general vocabulary for personal difficulty, social disadvantage, or emotional injury.[32] The result was an increasingly therapeutic model of social life in which harm and healing became political obligations.

The individual, once conceived as the bearer of rights, gradually became the bearer of symptoms — symptoms the state was tacitly responsible to alleviate.

This shift marked the rise of the **administrative self**, a self defined not by its autonomy but by its need for ongoing support, adjustment, and care.

LEGACY

The therapeutic state did not aim to remake man through coercion or purification. Its ambitions were different — and in some ways deeper. Where Bolsheviks and Maoists sought to transform humanity through struggle and enforced ideology, the democratic world sought to reshape him through guidance, therapy, and expert management. The tools differed profoundly; the underlying presumption did not:

> Human behavior is malleable.
>
> It can be shaped.
>
> It should be shaped.

The therapeutic state embodied the engineering impulse in its gentlest form — not by extending power into new domains,

---

[32] The medicalization of trauma accelerated after the inclusion of Post-Traumatic Stress Disorder in the *DSM-III* (1980). The broadened diagnostic framework helped popularize concepts such as emotional injury, micro-trauma, and "triggering" in schools, workplaces, and media.

but by changing the manner in which those domains were governed. What earlier revolutionary regimes controlled through fear and compulsion, the therapeutic state addressed through normalization, psychological framing, and appeals to care.

This marked a new phase in the age of the makeable man: the internalization of governance — the management of the psyche. [33]

---

[33] Scholars such as Nikolas Rose have examined the rise of what he terms "psychological citizenship", in which individuals come to relate to the state through categories of risk, vulnerability, and well-being, rather than through classical liberal notions of autonomy, responsibility, and civic duty. In this framework, governance operates increasingly through the management of subjectivity and self-regulation rather than through law alone.

Chapter 14
Technocracy and the Algorithmic Citizen

By the late twentieth century, modern societies faced a puzzle older than politics: how to govern complex populations without resorting to coercion. Liberal democracies, wary of totalitarian ideologies and haunted by the failures of revolutionary engineering, turned away from the language of purification and destiny. Yet they did not abandon the ambition to improve society. They simply adopted new instruments.

Instead of class struggle or cultural revolution, they embraced **expertise**.

Instead of ideology, **information**.

Instead of force, **incentive** and **design**.

Where earlier ages believed that knowledge could liberate, the modern administrative imagination believed that knowledge could **optimize**. And optimization required measurement. Once behavior could be measured, it could be predicted; once predicted, it could be shaped; once shaped, it could be governed.

Technocracy emerged from this progression — not as a conspiracy or an ideology, but as the natural outcome of a society that had grown confident in the capacity of science to manage life. The engineer's mindset, once applied to machines and factories, now applied to populations.

A new archetype entered political life: — the algorithmic citizen — a person understood as a set of behavioral patterns, risk factors, incentive structures, and decision tendencies, all of which could be subtly guided toward socially desirable outcomes.
34

---

34 Recent scholarship examines how digital infrastructures transform citizens into data subjects whose behaviors are predicted and shaped by algorithmic systems. Key works include Shoshana Zuboff's *The Age of*

The dream of the scientific state had returned, but in more ordinary clothing — the hum of administration rather than the noise of extraordinary authority.

THE RISE OF ADMINISTRATIVE REASON

The managerial revolution of the mid-twentieth century transformed private corporations, public bureaucracies, and national economies. Taylorism had once optimized factory labor; its descendants sought to optimize everything.

Governments hired economists, statisticians, psychologists, and systems theorists. Decision-making models proliferated. Forecasting became an administrative virtue. Policy ceased to be a contest of philosophical principles; it became an exercise in *solving problems* using tools borrowed from science.

In this environment, data acquired political force. It promised neutrality, objectivity, and above all *predictability*. Elections could deliver preferences. Data could deliver control.[35]

Public administration found itself increasingly guided by models — of economic behavior, social mobility, family structure, demographic change, urban design, and educational performance. Each model suggested an intervention; each intervention implied a desired outcome.

Surveillance Capitalism (2019), Frank Pasquale's *The Black Box Society* (2015), and Virginia Eubanks's *Automating Inequality* (2018), which analyze digital scoring, personalization, and automated decision-making in everyday life. Major institutions — including the OECD, the World Bank, and the Pew Research Center — have published reports on algorithmic governance, risk scoring, and behavioral prediction. Earlier antecedents appear in mid-twentieth-century work on decision theory and cybernetics, notably that of Herbert Simon and Norbert Wiener.

[35] Analyses of twentieth-century administrative rationality appear in Walter Lippmann's *Public Opinion* (1922) and James Burnham's *The Managerial Revolution* (1941), both of which anticipated the rise of expert-driven governance and the replacement of ideological authority with technical problem-solving.

The logic, once again, was simple:
    If you can predict behavior, you can guide it.
    If you can guide behavior, you can govern it.

Policy became less a matter of persuasion and more a matter of architecting environments in which citizens would choose what the experts believed they ought to choose.

BEHAVIORAL ECONOMICS AND THE SCIENCE OF PREDICTING CHOICE

In the 1970s and 1980s, psychology entered economics through the work of Daniel Kahneman and Amos Tversky. Human beings were revealed not as rational actors but as predictable ones — prone to cognitive biases, default tendencies, and systematic errors.

Governments quickly grasped the implications. If choices were predictable, they were also designable.

Behavioral economics introduced the idea of the **nudge**: a gentle modification of the environment that made one option easier, safer, cheaper, or more visible than another — without restricting freedom. A person could choose otherwise, but only with effort. [36]

Defaults replaced mandates. Recommendations replaced rules. Optimization replaced command.

The principle was elegant: **freedom preserved, outcomes guided.**

Yet beneath the elegance lay a deeper shift. The citizen had become a *variable*, a predictable reaction to structured incentives. Policy no longer addressed the soul or the conscience or the

---

[36] Daniel Kahneman and Amos Tversky's work on decision heuristics in the 1970s and 1980s provided the foundation for modern behavioral economics. Their findings later influenced public policy through "nudge" frameworks popularized by Richard Thaler and Cass Sunstein in *Nudge* (2008).

intellect; it addressed the decision-making machinery of the individual mind.

The therapeutic state treated citizens as patients. The technocratic state treated them as behavioral systems.

DIGITAL PATERNALISM AND THE SOFT ARCHITECTURE OF CONTROL

With the rise of the internet and later the smartphone, the scale of behavioral data expanded beyond anything imagined by the early technocrats. What governments once measured in broad aggregates could now be measured at the level of individual lives, in real time — search histories, location traces, click patterns, consumption rhythms, social interactions, sleep cycles, attention spans, and emotional cues.

The early twenty-first century saw the emergence of large-scale digital behavioral data. Platforms measured user interaction patterns at unprecedented resolution that enabled forms of personalization and behavioral adjustment impossible before.

Data turned human behavior into a map — one that could be analyzed, segmented, and predicted. If the behavioral economists had revealed how people chose, the digital infrastructure revealed *when*, *where*, *why*, and *with whom*.

This inaugurated a new form of governance: digital paternalism. Platforms optimized engagement. Advertisers optimized persuasion. Administrators optimized compliance. Health systems optimized lifestyle. Financial systems optimized spending and saving. Navigation apps optimized movement. Media systems optimized attention.

The citizen became the center of a personalized environment calibrated to shape choices long before those choices reached consciousness.

This was not tyranny. It was design.

Where Mao had demanded perpetual purification, the digital environment demanded **perpetual adjustment** — of preferences, habits, desires, and risk profiles. The individual navigated a world subtly arranged to reduce undesirable behaviors and promote desirable ones.

Freedom remained. But it was increasingly exercised within architectures built by others.

THE RETURN OF JACOBINISM — BY OTHER MEANS

The Jacobins believed that citizens could be purified through virtue and reason; the technocrats believed that citizens could be improved through information and optimization. The kinship was not ideological but structural.

Jacobinism sought to manufacture virtue. Technocracy sought to manufacture outcomes.

Both assumed that human behavior could be intentionally shaped. Both elevated experts — philosophers then, data scientists now. Both believed that society could be rationally redesigned. Both dissolved the old distinction between governing and improving.

But where the Jacobins enforced through terror, the technocrats enforce through **friction**:
> a delayed notification,
> a changed default option,
> a recommended route,
> a filtered feed,
> a flagged post.

Behavior is influenced not by fear of punishment, but by the architecture of everyday life. The ideological revolutions of the past reshaped society by force. The digital revolutions of the present reshape society by calibration.

THE ALGORITHMIC CITIZEN

The citizen of the algorithmic age is not merely a participant in democracy; he is a **subject of dataflows**. His preferences are analyzed, his risks assessed, his behaviors predicted, his attention monitored. Governments, corporations, digital platforms, financial systems, and administrative institutions all interact with him through layers of computational mediation. Long before the state reaches him as a citizen, the marketplace reaches him as a consumer, shaping his choices through continuous measurement, personalization, and design.

He is not coerced, but guided. Not commanded, but nudged. Not censored, but filtered. Not punished, but optimized.

The algorithmic citizen still votes, speaks, buys, travels, and chooses. But each choice takes place within an environment tuned to influence his behavior — gently, invisibly, pervasively.

In earlier centuries, authority acted upon the body. In revolutionary regimes, authority acted upon the mind. In the digital world, authority acts upon **the conditions of choice**.

This marks the completion of a long arc in the age of the makeable man: human nature is no longer confronted or overridden; it is accepted as given and then strategically exploited.

LEGACY

Technocracy did not set out to engineer the human being. It merely sought to solve problems. But in solving problems, it turned *people* into problems to be solved.

Its interventions were modest, reasonable, and therapeutic — and for that very reason, widely accepted. The engineering impulse, stripped of violence and clothed in expertise, embedded itself into the ordinary machinery of life. It did not demand loyalty or confession or revolutionary purity. It required only cooperation with systems designed for one's own good.

In this sense, technocracy is the gentlest descendant of Jacobinism. It replaces terror with optimization, ideology with data, coercion with guidance, purification with calibration. It asks not for sacrifice but for compatibility.

The age of the makeable man had entered its algorithmic phase.

The next part of this book will explore the digital culmination of this transformation — the emergence of systems that not only predict human behavior but begin to anticipate, preempt, and shape it. The goal will no longer be to produce the perfected human being, nor even the compliant one, but the predictable one.

Chapter 15
Silicon Valley and the New Utopians

In earlier centuries, revolutions sought to remake society. In the twentieth century, ideologies sought to remake human nature. In the algorithmic age, a new ambition arises: to remake the human being by technical means, voluntarily, continuously, and indefinitely.

This ambition emerged most vividly in the constellation of ideas surrounding Silicon Valley — not the place so much as the worldview. It is a vision that blends Enlightenment optimism, American pragmatism, cybernetic theory, and market confidence into a single proposition: Humanity is improvable, and technology is the instrument.

Where the Jacobins of a purified citizen, and Mao dreamed of a perfect revolutionary, the new utopians dream of an upgraded human: longer-lived, more intelligent, more rational, more efficient, more benevolent — a creature of software, supplements, metrics, and self-intervention.

If earlier movements tried to transform mankind by force, the new utopians try to transform him by design, with **the engineer as philosopher–king**.

THE NEW UTOPIAN TEMPERAMENT

The entrepreneurs, transhumanists, rationalists, biohackers, effective altruists, and techno-optimists who populate the intellectual ecosystem around Silicon Valley differ markedly in method and demeanor, but they share a common anthropology: **Human nature** is not a boundary; it **is a beta version**.

This is the new utopian temperament — confident, empirical, impatient with limits, enchanted by iteration. It is a worldview shaped less by Rousseau's politics than by the logic of the start-up:

> Identify a bottleneck.
> Build a prototype.
> Optimize the system.
> Scale the solution.
> Replace the old model entirely.

Applied to software, this process produces innovation. Applied to human life, it produces a new metaphysics.

To the new utopians, the self becomes something to upgrade. Biology becomes a platform. Cognition becomes computational. Morality becomes optimization under constraints. And society becomes a set of systems waiting for refactoring.

It is engineering raised to the level of philosophy.

THE TRANSHUMANIST DREAM

Transhumanism extends the Enlightenment dream of progress into the realm of biology. While eugenics had sought to improve the human stock by altering heredity, transhumanism seeks to improve the human type by transcending heredity altogether. [37]

Life extension, cryonics, neural implants, genetic modification, cognitive enhancement, and human-machine symbiosis all rest on a single conviction: **evolution is too slow, humanity can accelerate it**.

---

[37] For representative expressions of this outlook, see Nick Bostrom, *Superintelligence: Paths, Dangers, Strategies* (Oxford University Press, 2014); Ray Kurzweil, *The Singularity Is Near* (Viking, 2005); and Max More, "The Philosophy of Transhumanism" (in *The Transhumanist Reader*, 2013). These works articulate the view that human biological limits — including aging, cognition, and physical constraint — may be intentionally surpassed through technological intervention, replacing inherited conditions with engineered ones.

This ambition is not framed as domination but as liberation from disease, frailty, aging, and the contingency of natural selection. What the Enlightenment had promised through education and reason, transhumanism now promises through biotechnology and computation.

The deeper impulse is familiar: to take command of the conditions under which the human being exists.

Where eugenics had tried to design better generations, transhumanism tries to design better selves.

EFFECTIVE ALTRUISM AND THE OPTIMIZATION OF MORALITY

Another strand of the new utopian movement seeks not to upgrade bodies but to **optimize goodness**. Effective altruism, born from analytic philosophy and nourished by the wealth of the tech sector, reframed ethics as a calculus of outcomes. [38] If the goal is to do the most good, then emotion, intuition, and tradition must yield to models, metrics, probabilities, and expected-value calculations.

The old moral vocabulary — virtue, duty, honor — becomes insufficient. The new vocabulary is quantitative: impact, marginal return, tractability, global utility.

This is moral engineering.

It is animated by humanitarian intent, but governed by the logic of optimization. Even the future becomes a domain for calculation: the well-being of generations yet unborn becomes a variable in present decision-making. Few movements in history

---

[38] See William MacAskill, *Doing Good Better: How Effective Altruism Can Help You Make a Difference* (Avery, 2015); Peter Singer, *The Life You Can Save* (Random House, 2009); and Toby Ord, *The Precipice* (Hachette, 2020). These works frame ethics in explicitly quantitative terms, emphasizing expected value, cost-effectiveness, and the maximization of aggregate well-being across populations and time.

have extended their moral horizon so far — or attempted to do so with such technical precision.

In this effort to refactor ethics, the new utopians echo an ancient pattern: the belief that human conduct can be rationalized into a system directed toward perfection.

RATIONALISM AND THE CULT OF COGNITION

A parallel development arises in the rationalist communities that orbit Silicon Valley. For them, the obstacle to improving humanity is not biology or morality, but cognition itself. Biases, heuristics, mental blind spots, and emotional distortions corrupt judgment. The goal becomes the re-engineering of belief.

Where behaviorists sought to condition actions, the rationalists seek to condition assumptions:
> belief updating,
> probabilistic reasoning,
> epistemic hygiene,
> "debugging" thought.

This is selfhood treated as a codebase — editable, patchable, improvable.

The Cartesian dream of clarity[39] returns: the hope that reason, properly purified of error, tradition, and distortion, can arrive at reliable truth by method alone. But now it is armed with

---

[39] The "Cartesian dream of clarity" refers to the epistemic aspiration articulated by René Descartes to ground knowledge in methodical certainty — reason purified of tradition, authority, and ambiguity, arriving at truth through systematic doubt and clear principles. In this vision, error is not a condition to be interpreted, but a defect to be eliminated by proper method. Modern appeals to calibration, optimization, and cognitive purification echo this aspiration, even as they replace certainty with continuous adjustment.

Bayesian statistics[40] and machine-learning[41] metaphors — echoing earlier psychological instruments that privileged calibration over understanding. Beliefs are not interpreted; they are adjusted. Error is not examined for meaning; it is corrected through updating.

The rationalists pursue a cultivated mind, purified not by ideology but by calibration. Where Mao demanded ideological purity, the rationalists demand cognitive accuracy — a quieter, but structurally similar, effort to align the mind with a normative model of correctness.

SILICON VALLEY AS A POLITICAL IMAGINATION

These movements are not fringe curiosities. They shape how entire sectors of society now understand the future.

For many in Silicon Valley and its cultural orbit, the engineer replaces the philosopher, the founder replaces the legislator, and the start-up replaces the revolution. The world is no longer changed through mass mobilization or ideological struggle, but through products, platforms, and protocols.

This worldview holds that:

      problems are puzzles waiting for solutions;

---

[40] Bayesian statistics refers to a family of probabilistic methods in which beliefs or predictions are continuously updated as new evidence becomes available. Rather than seeking certainty, Bayesian reasoning treats knowledge as provisional and revisable, emphasizing calibration over finality. In contemporary technocratic and algorithmic contexts, this approach has become a dominant metaphor for rationality itself: not the discovery of truth, but the ongoing adjustment of confidence in response to data.

[41] Machine learning refers to a class of computational methods that identify patterns in data and adjust behavior or predictions through repeated feedback rather than explicit rules. In this framework, intelligence is modeled not as judgment or understanding, but as optimization — continuous refinement of outputs to better match desired outcomes. As a metaphor for rationality, machine learning emphasizes calibration, responsiveness, and performance over comprehension or final explanation.

institutions are legacy code;

norms are outdated interfaces;

and human limitations are merely engineering constraints.

The underlying impulse is not malice but impatience — impatience with fragility, tragedy, finitude, and the slow pace of history. The desire is to build something better, faster, smarter, scalable.

Yet beneath this optimism lies a continuity older than the digital age: the belief that human life can be consciously redesigned. Saint-Simon had imagined a society governed by industrialists and engineers. Silicon Valley inherits that dream — only now with capital, computation, and reach on a civilizational scale.

THE LIMITS OF OPTIMIZATION

But human life does not yield easily to algorithmic refinement any more than it did for the harsher and directly coercive attempts. The engineer's mindset, which excels in controlled systems, falters in the unpredictability of lived experience. Optimizing a machine differs from optimizing a man.

Human beings resist refactoring. Their desires contradict one another. Their values cannot be reduced to a single metric. Their identities shift under the pressure of circumstance. Their flourishing cannot be plotted on a dashboard.

The new utopians assume that improvement is always possible. History suggests that improvement is always complicated.

Earlier technological efforts to optimize the human being relied on instruments that were necessarily slow and retrospective. Psychological tools such as personality inventories and aptitude tests classified individuals by comparing their responses to statistically normed populations. [42] Meaning was inferred from correlation rather than understanding, and conclusions depended on the accumulation of data across time. By the time stable patterns emerged, the social conditions that produced them had often changed. Norms drifted. Context shifted. Instruments required continual revision simply to remain relevant.

Contemporary computational systems appear to overcome this limitation. They adapt in real time, recalibrate continuously, and respond instantly to behavior. Feedback loops close rapidly. Correlation no longer lags behind action.

Yet speed does not resolve the deeper problem. These systems remain blind to meaning. They register patterns without understanding purpose, and they optimize responses without grasping causes. Faster calibration does not produce wisdom; it accelerates intervention. Instead of lagging behind human life, optimization now acts upon it before meaning can stabilize — shaping choices as it measures them. The problem is no longer obsolescence, but premature closure.

The Enlightenment dreamed of a rational humanity. Silicon Valley dreams of an optimized one. Both underestimate the depth of the human condition.

LEGACY

The new utopians did not set out to remake humanity through domination or revolution. Their ambitions were humanitarian, rational, and often admirable. Yet the structure of their thought repeats an ancient pattern: If human nature can be

---

[42] Instruments such as the Minnesota Multiphasic Personality Inventory (MMPI), developed in the mid-twentieth century, exemplify this shift in psychological reasoning. Rather than interpreting meaning or intention, such tools classify individuals by statistically normed response patterns, treating personality as something to be measured, compared, and recalibrated rather than understood in moral or narrative terms.

improved, then it should be; if it can be redesigned, then it must be.

Silicon Valley offers the gentlest utopianism in the long lineage of Western attempts to perfect man — gentle not because its goals are small, but because its tools are subtle: code, metrics, models, enhancements, and iterative design.

It replaces the revolutionary's hammer with the engineer's prototype. It replaces the cadre with the founder. It replaces the commissariat with the accelerator. It replaces the political catechism with the product roadmap.

In this way, the Algorithmic Citizen introduced in the previous chapter finds his voluntary counterpart. Where technocracy treated the citizen as a behavioral system to be guided, optimized, and calibrated, the new utopians invite him to become the engineer of his own design. Metrics once imposed externally are now embraced internally. Optimization shifts from governance to identity.

What began as administration becomes aspiration. The system no longer needs to compel adjustment, because adjustment has become a personal project. The Algorithmic Citizen is no longer only managed; he is self-managed — quantified, optimized, and iterated from within.

The aspiration remains the same: to build a human being better suited to the future than the past.

What once governed the Algorithmic Citizen from without is now **internalized as a digital self**. External goals, metrics, and optimization regimes are no longer merely imposed; they are mirrored, adopted, and amplified from within. Governance gives way to self-regulation, and the logic of the system becomes a way of understanding oneself.

A **new kind of problem arises**, one not of control but of **unsettled meaning**. When the self is rendered measurable, comparable, and improvable without limit, questions once answered by tradition, faith, or philosophy return in altered form: Who am I, apart from my metrics? What remains when optimization never ends? And what becomes of purpose when improvement replaces orientation?

What earlier forms of self-improvement shared — whether religious, artistic, professional, or philosophical — was a relatively stable point of orientation. One improved oneself *toward* something: salvation, beauty, mastery, truth, or excellence within a recognizable tradition. The end preceded the method.

The digital self operates differently. Its **standards are not inherited but generated**, not stable but continuously updated, not shared but personalized. External systems translate social expectations into algorithmic signals — rankings, scores, engagement metrics, reputational cues — which are then internalized and acted upon. Improvement no longer aims at a fixed conception of the good; it responds to shifting feedback. The question "toward what?" is replaced by "according to what performs better now?"

Part V:
The Modern Crisis of Meaning

Chapter 16
The Return of Empty Labels

Modern public life is saturated with language and starved of meaning. Words are spoken with confidence, even urgency, yet they increasingly fail to clarify what is actually being said. Terms are stretched, intensified, and repurposed to convey feeling rather than definition. Precision gives way to impact. Description yields to expression. This development did not originate in the present moment. It has been observed for decades, though its pace and scope have accelerated markedly in recent years.

This is not new at the level of casual speech. Ordinary people have always been imprecise with language. What *is* new is the collapse of a shared reference class. The institutions once responsible for stabilizing meaning — education, journalism, scholarship, law, and professional communication — now participate in the same drift. Words are no longer disciplined by definition; they are rewarded for resonance.[43]

The result is a general corruption in the use of language across media, culture, and public discourse. The effect reveals itself most dramatically in political discourse, where the consequences become impossible to ignore.

Political debate suffers most from this degradation of language because it depends most heavily on shared meaning. Governance requires distinctions, limits, and proportional judgment. When language loses its descriptive anchor, political disagreement becomes intense but incoherent — charged with emotion, stripped of structure. It is not so much that something

---

[43] On the degradation of public language and the substitution of rhetoric for meaning, see *Politics and the English Language* (1946); *The Tyranny of Words* (1938); and *The Image* (1961). Each examines how language shifts from description toward persuasion, abstraction, and emotional effect.

has gone wrong with politics, but with the language used to conduct it.

WHEN WORDS OUTLIVE THE IDEAS THAT GAVE THEM MEANING

Modern political discourse is loud, urgent, and emotionally charged — yet strangely hollow. Familiar terms are invoked with confidence and force, but rarely with precision. *Fascist, socialist, autocrat, radical, democracy, freedom* circulate constantly, yet they no longer seem to clarify anything. They function less as descriptions than as signals, less as concepts than as instruments of alignment and accusation.

This is not simply a problem of bad education or media distortion. It is a structural consequence of the modern age itself. Political language has not merely been abused; it has been unmoored.

WORDS BORN IN HISTORY, USED WITHOUT IT

Political terms are not abstract inventions. They arise from specific historical conditions, institutional arrangements, and philosophical commitments. *Fascism* emerged from post–First World War Italy, defined by corporatism, mythic nationalism, and mass mobilization under a single-party state. *Socialism* arose from nineteenth-century critiques of industrial capitalism, rooted in theories of labor, class, and material distribution. *Autocracy* once referred to particular forms of centralized, unaccountable rule. *Radical* originally meant a desire to return to roots, not a willingness to accept rapid change for its own sake.[44] [45]

---

[44] Throughout this book, the term "radical" is used primarily in its modern sense to denote far-reaching or transformative change, rather than in its original sense of change directed at the root (*radix*).

[45] For original definitions and historical usage, see the Oxford English Dictionary and Encyclopaedia Britannica, both of which trace the

These words once described systems — coherent, if contested, arrangements of power, economy, and authority. They referred to structures, not attitudes; to doctrines, not emotions.

In the modern age, they have been detached from those origins.

They now float freely, applied to personalities, policies, moods, and even individual behaviors. A school board decision becomes "fascist." A tax policy becomes "socialist." A procedural executive action becomes "autocratic." A cultural disagreement becomes "radicalization."

The result is not clarity, but inflation.

THE THERAPEUTIC TURN AND THE COLLAPSE OF DESCRIPTION

The decay of political language coincides with the rise of politics as therapy.

As governance shifted from regulating conduct to *managing feelings*, political categories followed suit. Words that once described institutional realities now describe *psychological states*. They signal threat, offense, safety, or harm rather than structure or intent.

To call something "fascist" is no longer to identify a governing model; it is to express fear or moral revulsion. To label a policy "socialist" is often to indicate anxiety about control, not a theory of ownership. **Political language becomes diagnostic rather than descriptive** — an expression of distress rather than analysis.

---

development of political terms such as "fascism," "socialism," "autocracy," and "radical" within their proper historical and institutional contexts. These sources preserve the distinction between formal systems of governance and the more generalized or metaphorical uses common in contemporary discourse.

This transformation aligns perfectly with the therapeutic state described in the previous chapters. When politics becomes a matter of emotional regulation, language becomes a tool of *affect* rather than *understanding*.

Words cease to explain the world. They exist to manage reactions to it.

THE LOSS OF SHARED REFERENCE POINTS

Meaning requires shared reference.

In earlier eras, political disagreement still occurred within a common conceptual framework. Liberals and conservatives, monarchists and republicans, socialists and capitalists argued fiercely — but they generally agreed on what the terms *meant*. Conflict occurred over values, not definitions.

That consensus has collapsed.

In a society where human nature itself is seen as malleable, language loses its anchor. If identities, norms, and institutions are all subject to redesign, then the words that describe them cannot stabilize. Terms become provisional, flexible, and opportunistic — adjusted to immediate rhetorical needs.

This is not accidental. It is the linguistic expression of the makeable-man worldview.

If everything is adjustable, so is meaning.

LABELS AS INSTRUMENTS OF CONTROL

Once words lose descriptive content, they gain a new function.

They become tools for classification.

To label is to sort. To sort is to position. To position is to justify response — exclusion, sanction, correction, or "intervention." In this way, empty labels serve the same function once served by class categories, diagnostic terms, or behavioral profiles.

They identify *who must be managed*.

In the absence of shared meaning, labels operate performatively. They do not describe reality; they *create* it — by assigning moral status, social risk, or political legitimacy. A person is not debated; he is labeled. **Once labeled, the conversation is effectively over.**[46]

This is why modern political disputes feel unresolved and interminable. They are not disagreements about policy or structure; they are conflicts over identity classification. Each side speaks past the other, armed with words that no longer point to the same things.

WHY THE LABELS RETURN, EMPTY

The emptiness of modern political language is not a sign of ignorance alone. It is a symptom of something deeper.

As the older moral and philosophical frameworks recede — religion, natural law, shared tradition — politics inherits responsibilities it cannot fulfill. It must now provide meaning, identity, and purpose. Language stretches to meet these demands, and in doing so, breaks.

The labels return because they are needed. They are empty because they are overburdened.

They must explain too much, condemn too quickly, and unify too many anxieties at once.

THE COST OF INCOHERENCE

When language fails, power does not.

The inability to name political realities clearly does not produce neutrality; it produces confusion — and confusion

---

[46] On the performative and classificatory function of language in modern social systems, see *The Sociological Imagination* (1959) and *Language, Truth and Logic* (1936). Both address the relationship between language, classification, and the construction of social reality.

invites management. In a world where words no longer clarify, authority shifts to those who claim expertise, data, or moral urgency rather than argument.

The loss of meaning becomes a governance problem.

This prepares the ground for the final transformation examined in this part of the book: the inward turn, where politics no longer argues about society, but administers the soul.

The next chapter will examine how radicalism itself becomes therapeutic — how political movements increasingly define themselves not by programs or structures, but by claims of injury, healing, and moral restoration.

When words can no longer describe the world, they are used to treat it.

Chapter 17
Radicalism as Therapy:
The Politics of the Soul

The previous chapters traced a gradual but decisive shift in modern governance. The state no longer understood its primary task as ruling citizens through law alone, but as improving them through expertise. Politics softened into administration, administration into therapy. What began as public policy increasingly addressed not behavior but well-being, not conduct but inner life.

At the same time, the citizen himself changed. As the algorithmic age matured, external systems of guidance, measurement, and optimization were internalized. The individual learned to see himself as a project — quantified, monitored, improvable. The therapeutic state and the digital self converged, producing a new moral landscape in which governance and self-regulation became difficult to distinguish.

Language did not remain untouched by this transformation. As shared political terms lost their descriptive precision, they did not vanish. They migrated inward. Political conflict turned away from institutions and laws and toward feelings, identities, and psychic states. Disagreement came to be experienced less as error than as injury, opposition less as argument than as harm.

In this new register, power no longer presents itself primarily as authority to be obeyed or claims to be debated. It appears as care. Moral disagreement is reframed as pathology. Resistance becomes a symptom. And the work of politics shifts from persuading citizens to treating souls.

What follows is not a history of ideology, but a diagnosis of a transformation: the moment when radicalism ceased to speak chiefly in the language of justice and began to speak in the language of therapy.

THE POLITICS OF THE SOUL

Modern radicalism no longer presents itself primarily as a theory of power or a program of governance. It presents itself as a form of care.

Its language is therapeutic. Its justifications are psychological. Its authority rests not on doctrine alone, but on claims about harm, healing, trauma, identity, and emotional safety. Political disagreement is no longer framed as a contest of ideas, but as a diagnosis. To **dissent is not merely to be wrong; it is to be unwell**.

This marks a decisive shift in the nature of radical politics.

Earlier radical movements — Jacobin, Bolshevik, Maoist— sought to remake the human being through overt instruments: terror, purification, reeducation, and force. Contemporary radicalism operates through a subtler register. It seeks not obedience, but affirmation; not conformity, but validation; not submission, but confession. Power no longer announces itself as authority. It appears as care.

FROM IDEOLOGY TO DIAGNOSIS

In the classical political tradition, disagreement implied error, interest, or vice. One might be mistaken, corrupt, or immoral — but one remained a rational agent capable of persuasion or resistance.

The therapeutic turn alters this assumption. Political disagreement is reinterpreted as a symptom rather than a stance. Beliefs are no longer arguments to be answered; they are expressions of identity, trauma, or pathology to be treated.

Thus political language migrates into clinical categories:[47]
> disagreement becomes *harm*
> opposition becomes *violence*
> dissent becomes *trauma*
> persuasion becomes *manipulation*
> conviction becomes *radicalization*

The debate is no longer over what is true or just, but over what is safe or unsafe, healthy or unhealthy. Politics adopts the posture of therapy, and the citizen becomes a patient.

THE MORAL AUTHORITY OF SUFFERING

Therapeutic radicalism derives its legitimacy from suffering — real, perceived, inherited, or anticipated. Claims are validated not by coherence or evidence, but by proximity to pain. To speak from suffering is to speak with authority; to question suffering is to commit an offense.[48]

This is not cynicism. Much of the suffering invoked is genuine. But the political use of suffering transforms it into a moral credential. Identity becomes a proxy for truth. Experience replaces argument. And moral authority shifts from what one can justify to what one has endured.

Once suffering becomes the highest form of legitimacy, politics acquires a new aim: not to reconcile interests or establish justice, but to affirm identities and manage emotional states. The task of governance becomes psychological regulation.

---

[47] For analyses of the therapeutic framing of language and politics, see *The Triumph of the Therapeutic* (1966); *The Culture of Narcissism* (1979); and *The Coddling of the American Mind* (2018), which document the increasing use of psychological and clinical categories to interpret disagreement, harm, and social conflict.

[48] On the rise of suffering as a basis of moral authority, see *The Victimhood Culture* (2018); and *What's Our Problem?* (2023), both of which describe the shift from honor and dignity frameworks toward identity and harm-based moral claims in contemporary culture.

THE INWARD TURN OF POWER

This development completes a long arc traced throughout this book. Where earlier regimes enforced order through direct control of bodies, modern regimes govern the conditions that shape behavior. Where technocratic systems guided action, therapeutic systems shape identity. Where authority once operated externally, it now operates internally. Power turns inward.

The citizen is encouraged — often sincerely — to examine his beliefs, language, emotions, and reactions for traces of harm. He learns to self-monitor, self-correct, and self-censor.[49] The boundary between moral improvement and political compliance dissolves.

The result is a new kind of obedience: voluntary, internalized, and moralized.

RADICALISM WITHOUT A TELOS

Classical radicalism sought to return society to its roots. Modern therapeutic radicalism lacks even that orientation. It does not aim at a final order, a resolved justice, or a stable vision of the good. Its project is **perpetual intervention**.

Because identity is fluid, harm is ongoing, and trauma is recursive, the work is never finished. There is always another bias to uncover, another language to revise, another structure to interrogate. Politics becomes an endless process of self-examination without resolution.

In this sense, radicalism becomes therapy without discharge.

---

[49] This inward turn of power echoes earlier analyses such as *Discipline and Punish* (1975), which described the internalization of surveillance and control within modern institutions, though the present argument extends this dynamic into the therapeutic and psychological domain.

THE SOUL AS POLITICAL TERRITORY

What is novel is not that politics concerns itself with the inner life. That is as old as Plato. What is novel is the assumption that the inner life is politically actionable at scale.

The soul — once the domain of philosophy, religion, and art — becomes a site of policy. Emotional states are categorized, tracked, and managed. Moral language is medicalized. And political legitimacy rests increasingly on the promise of psychological safety rather than civic order.

The manufactured man no longer needs to be coerced. He needs to be *helped*.

THE COST OF THERAPEUTIC POLITICS

Therapeutic radicalism promises compassion, but it produces fragility. It promises inclusion, but it generates exclusion through moral diagnosis. It promises healing, but it removes the conditions under which genuine disagreement — and therefore genuine agency — can exist.

When politics becomes therapy, dissent becomes pathology. And when dissent is pathologized, **freedom collapses into compliance disguised as care**.

It governs not by force, but by shaping affect — what feels safe, harmful, acceptable, or intolerable.

This is not tyranny in the classical sense. It is something more subtle, more intimate, and more difficult to resist: a form of self-imposed rule, internalized by individuals and administered through the state.

TOWARD THE AUTOCRAT OF THE SELF

The next chapter completes this inward turn.

If radicalism treats the soul as a site of intervention, the manufactured man becomes the manager of his own interior regime. Authority no longer needs to be imposed, because it has been internalized.

The age of the manufactured man reaches its most intimate form. Not the state over the self, but the self as the state.

Chapter 18
The Manufactured Man and the Autocrat of the Self

The transformation traced in the preceding chapters does not culminate in a new regime, a new ideology, or even a new system of governance. It culminates in **a new relationship between the individual and himself**.

By the time power has migrated inward — when language signals *feeling* rather than *meaning*, when disagreement is diagnosed rather than debated, and when improvement replaces orientation — the traditional figure of the autocrat is no longer required. Authority has found a more reliable home.

It resides in the self.

This is the arrival of the manufactured man.

From External Authority to Internal Rule

Earlier ages understood power as something exercised over people. Kings ruled subjects. States governed citizens. Even revolutionary regimes, for all their ambition, still relied on external instruments: laws, decrees, surveillance, punishment, reeducation.

What distinguishes the present condition is not greater force, but greater intimacy.

The manufactured man governs himself according to standards he did not create, in pursuit of goals he did not define, using metrics he did not invent. He evaluates his own worth, calibrates his own behavior, disciplines his own speech, and monitors his own thoughts — often sincerely, often voluntarily, and often in the name of virtue.

No policeman is required when the rules have been internalized. No censor is needed when the self anticipates correction. No tyrant is necessary when the subject has become his own administrator.

This is not the abolition of authority. It is its perfection.

THE LOGIC OF SELF-GOVERNANCE

The autocrat of the self does not issue commands. He manages processes.

He asks:

> Is this belief acceptable?
> Is this reaction appropriate?
> Is this language safe?
> Is this identity aligned?
> Is this behavior optimized?

These questions are framed as moral concern or personal growth, but they function as regulatory checks. The self becomes a site of continuous evaluation, comparison, and adjustment.

What once arrived as law now arrives as conscience — but a conscience shaped by external systems of measurement, validation, and approval. The line between moral judgment and administrative compliance dissolves.

The manufactured man is not compelled to think differently. He learns to evaluate himself differently. Regulation no longer arrives as command, but as self-assessment. Authority does not silence dissent; it teaches the individual to silence it himself, often sincerely and in the name of care.

The individual becomes **both ruler and ruled**.

MANUFACTURE WITHOUT FINALITY

This condition of the manufactured man described herein can be mistaken for a refined form of brainwashing. Both result in compliance, but the distinction in method is critical.

Brainwashing is coercive and episodic; it seeks to break resistance through force, fear, or deprivation. Self-governance operates continuously and voluntarily. It does not impose belief; it reshapes the criteria by which belief is judged.

But the manufactured man differs from classical reeducation in one crucial respect: **there is no endpoint**. In this respect, it bears a structural resemblance — not in violence, but in logic — to Maoist notions of perpetual self-revision, where the individual was never fully reformed but always subject to further correction. The manufactured man lives under a similar condition of endless adjustment, not enforced by terror, but sustained by internalized evaluation.

Earlier projects of human redesign, however destructive, still imagined completion. Eugenics sought a healthier population. Revolution sought a purified society. Technocracy sought stable optimization. Each aimed — however correctly or mistakenly — at a finished condition.

The manufactured man lives under perpetual revision. There is always another bias to uncover, another habit to refine, another metric to improve, another identity to reconfigure. Completion is neither promised nor permitted. Improvement is no longer a path toward a goal; it *is* the goal.

This absence of finality is not accidental. It is the logical consequence of a world without fixed orientation. When no enduring conception of the good anchors judgment, adjustment must continue indefinitely. The self cannot arrive, because arrival would imply a standard beyond optimization itself.

The autocrat of the self never abdicates.

FREEDOM REVISITED

In classical political thought, freedom meant freedom from arbitrary rule. In the modern administrative age, it meant freedom within managed systems.

In the present condition, freedom is redefined once more. It becomes the freedom to self-regulate.

But this self-regulation is not spontaneous. It is coaxed by structured incentives, feedback mechanisms, and normative signals informed by behavioral science and amplified by technology. The manufactured man experiences this not as oppression, but as agency. He "chooses" his constraints. He adopts his disciplines. He embraces his metrics. He experiences control as responsibility and compliance as care.

This is why resistance feels confused and fragmented. There is no obvious oppressor to confront. Power does not stand opposite the individual; it speaks in his own voice.

Earlier societies relied on visible, situational forms of influence. A collection plate passed visibly through a church, a public expectation in the work environment, a shared ritual or custom — all exerted pressure, but only in context. One could step outside the setting, and the demand receded. Influence had a beginning and an end.

The manufactured condition operates differently. The individual evaluates himself continuously, even in the absence of observers. He reconsiders a sentence before speaking, not because someone is watching, but because he has learned to anticipate judgment. He hesitates before selecting a film, a book, or a news source, not because it is forbidden, but because it may signal the wrong alignment. He moderates opinions expressed in private messages, professional settings, or internal thought, guided by an internalized sense of what will be rewarded, penalized, or recorded.

The difference is subtle but decisive. Earlier pressures were imposed from without and relieved by distance. This pressure is self-administered and uninterrupted. The individual becomes both monitor and monitored, enforcing norms even when no one else is present.

Freedom remains — but it is exercised under continuous self-evaluation.

What distinguishes this condition is not the disappearance of older forms of pressure, but the addition of a new one. Traditional constraints — law, custom, authority, and overt coercion — have not vanished. What has changed is that a new layer of self-evaluation now exists, ambient and always available, even in their absence.

This layer does not replace external constraint; it supplements it. It operates not by issuing commands, but by introducing **a pause** — a moment of internal checking — before speech, action, or even attention. The individual does not need to be stopped. He only needs to be made to reconsider.

The significance of this shift lies not in any single decision altered, but in the **cumulative effect of repeated self-correction**. Each adjustment appears minor, even prudent. But over time, the constant presence of the check reshapes what feels natural, sayable, and permissible. What yields once yields more easily again.

THE COST OF TOTAL INTERIORIZATION

The price of this arrangement is subtle but profound.

When authority becomes entirely internal, error becomes guilt. Disagreement becomes defect. Difference becomes risk. The self is never simply mistaken; it is misaligned. The moral life collapses into compliance with shifting norms that cannot be fully articulated or contested.

Meaning erodes not through prohibition, but **through exhaustion**.

The manufactured man is busy — optimizing, improving, adjusting — but increasingly uncertain why. He is active without orientation, disciplined without direction, and free without a horizon.

A Condition, Not a Conspiracy

It is important to say what this chapter does *not* claim. The manufactured man is not the product of a secret plot. He is not the victim of a single ideology. He is not the result of malice.

He is the outcome of ideas long in motion — about improvement, care, progress, safety, and human malleability — applied patiently, compassionately, and efficiently across generations.

The manufactured man is not imposed. He is produced.

Beyond the Manufactured Man

If this book has traced a movement — from the given human, to the makeable man, to the manufactured condition — it must now ask its final question.

What remains of freedom, meaning, and responsibility when governance has become internal, language has lost its anchor, and the self has become both project and authority?

That question does not admit of a programmatic answer. But it does require recognition.

The chapters that follow will not offer a solution, but a vantage point. Not a return, but a reckoning. Not a system, but a way of seeing.

To understand the manufactured man is not to reject him, nor to deny the achievements that produced him. It is to ask whether a human life governed by perpetual improvement — bounded everywhere yet completed nowhere — can still possess meaning. And whether a civilization that refuses final limits has quietly abandoned the very conditions under which a human being can say "enough," and mean it.

But first we will turn to some relatable examples of existence for the manufactured man.

Chapter 19
Examples of the Managed Self

By this point in the book, the reader may feel that something has shifted. Earlier chapters dealt in visible forces: institutions, doctrines, programs, revolutions, laws. Power announced itself plainly. Authority issued commands. Compliance was enforced through explicit mechanisms — police, courts, prisons, party structures, or public sanction. One could point to the source of pressure and name it.

Recent chapters may have been more difficult to grasp, not because they are weaker, but because the forces under examination are less overt. They do not present themselves as discrete actions or visible pressures, but as environments, incentives, and patterns that shape behavior indirectly and over time. They are distributed and indirect.

History trained us to recognize authority when it issued commands and imposed penalties, and to recognize power when it acted upon bodies and institutions. It did not train us to recognize authority when it reshapes incentives, reframes risk, and governs behavior through procedure rather than explicit force.

What follows does not advance a new argument. It turns instead to illustration. The purpose of this chapter is not to persuade, indict, or resolve, but to make a condition visible — one many readers have already encountered without fully articulating. The examples that follow are drawn deliberately from ordinary experience. Not from ideology or doctrine, but from routine practices; not from crises at first, but from everyday systems.

These illustrations are chosen precisely because they are unremarkable. They are familiar domains in which participation is expected, alignment is rewarded, and standing is continuously maintained rather than conclusively secured. Only after establishing this baseline will the chapter widen its scope, showing how the same architecture, already present in institutional life, becomes unmistakable when activated at scale under conditions of emergency.

THE CORPORATE TRAINING MACHINE

For many readers, the most familiar expression of modern authority is not found in courts, police stations, or legislatures, but in conference rooms, onboarding portals, and mandatory online modules. Corporate training has become one of the most pervasive — and least examined — forms of behavioral governance in contemporary life.

It is introduced without drama. Employees are informed that a training module is required, often annually, sometimes quarterly. The language is reassuring. This is not a punishment. It is not an accusation. It is presented as protection — for the company, certainly, but also for the individual. *This training exists for your benefit. It helps you navigate risk. It keeps everyone safe.*

The content rarely appeals to character. Courage is not named. Prudence appears only as compliance. Judgment is displaced by procedure. The employee is not asked what the right thing to do might be under conditions of uncertainty; he is shown which actions expose him to risk. Ethical reasoning recedes as risk management takes its place.

What is taught, above all, is not virtue, but avoidance.

Rules are framed less as expressions of the good than as safeguards against harm — harm to reputation, harm to career, harm to the institution. Ethical failure is defined not by wrongdoing as such, but by exposure. The operative question is no longer, *What ought one to do?* but *What could happen to you if this is handled incorrectly?*

This logic is reinforced structurally. Training modules conclude with attestations. The employee must acknowledge that the material has been reviewed, that the policies are understood, and that compliance is expected. The act of acknowledgment transfers responsibility downward. The system does not require conviction; it requires alignment.

None of this is framed as coercion. Participation is mandatory, but the tone remains therapeutic. The employee is not threatened; he is advised. Compliance is achieved not through fear of punishment, but through fear of consequence — vague, personal, and persistent.

The system operates continuously rather than episodically. There is no final final-exam, no completion of moral formation, **no point at which the subject is declared finished**. Training is renewed. Policies are revised. Expectations evolve. The individual remains permanently adjustable.

This is not an aberration of corporate life. It is a model.

Ethics versus Corporate Pragmatism

What modern institutions describe as "ethics training" represents a significant shift — not in moral aspiration, but in where responsibility is located. Corporate ethics programs emerged not as an extension of character formation, but as part of a growing compliance infrastructure. Their purpose was practical from the outset.

This shift took shape gradually. In the late 1980s and 1990s, ethics entered corporate life primarily as a defensive measure. Training programs, codes of conduct, and documentation systems were introduced to demonstrate diligence in the event of misconduct. In 1991, the U.S. Federal Sentencing Guidelines for Organizations explicitly rewarded companies that could show the existence of compliance programs and an "ethical culture." One could say that this was the birth of ethics as paperwork.

The early 2000s marked a second inflection point. High-profile corporate failures — Enron, WorldCom, Tyco — were followed by regulatory responses that emphasized traceability: who knew what, when they knew it, and what procedures were in place. Although subsequent legislation did not mandate ethics training explicitly, it made documentation central. Ethics became institutionalized as risk management.

What changed was not morality, but attribution. Previously, responsibility for employee conduct rested primarily with managers, mentorship, and organizational leadership, with escalation to formal mechanisms only in exceptional cases. In the newer model, responsibility is displaced downward. The company can now say, *We trained you. We informed you. You acknowledged the rules.* Ethical failure is reframed as individual deviation rather than systemic condition.

In this translation, ethics shifts from a matter of judgment to a matter of defensibility. The aim is no longer the formation of character, but the reduction of exposure. The individual is not asked to deliberate under uncertainty; he is trained to follow procedure. Trust is replaced by auditability.

This stands in contrast to the classical understanding of ethical life. In that tradition, ethics concerned the formation of character and the exercise of judgment. Virtue did not consist in rigid adherence to rules, but in proportion — the capacity to navigate between excess and deficiency. Courage, for example, was understood as a mean between cowardice and rashness; generosity, between stinginess and wastefulness. Ethical action required discernment, visibility, and the acceptance of personal risk.

From that perspective, the unqualified following of all rules and procedures would not have been praised as virtue, but regarded as a form of immoderation — a behavioral extreme.

What is rewarded in modern ethics training is not judgment, but **com**pliance; not character, but alignment.

This observation is not a criticism of what may be necessary for the functioning of large organizations. Rules, procedures, and compliance mechanisms serve practical purposes, and no complex institution could operate without them. The difficulty lies elsewhere. What is pragmatic at the level of the organization becomes mis-labeled when it is presented as moral formation at the level of the individual. Corporate risk management is quietly internalized as personal virtue.

Perhaps the most revealing feature of contemporary ethics training is the encouragement of anonymous reporting. Employees are instructed that if something appears improper, they should not confront it directly or resolve it openly. They should report it — safely, discreetly, without personal exposure. This is framed as responsibility and care.

Yet this removes precisely what classical ethics required: visibility, ownership, and risk. In an ethics of character, one stands openly for what one believes to be right and accepts the consequences of that judgment. In a system of compliance, **moral responsibility is transferred to process**. The individual does not act; he signals. He does not judge; he escalates. Courage is replaced by insulation.

In this way, organizational alignment quietly redefines what it means to be a "good" employee. Worth is no longer measured primarily by competence or responsibility borne, but by demonstrable conformity to approved procedures. Ethics becomes something one executes, acknowledges, and renews.

PERPETUAL TRAINING AND DISTRIBUTED RESPONSIBILITY

A defining feature of contemporary training regimes is their lack of completion. There is never enough training. Courses are renewed annually, often supplemented by new modules while previous requirements remain in force. Policies are revised, expanded, and reissued, frequently accompanied by attestations that the employee has reviewed and agrees to follow all rules set forth — regardless of their number, complexity, or continual modification.

The effect is not mastery, but permanent provisionality. The employee is never fully formed, never fully compliant, never finished. Ethical standing becomes something that must be continually re-earned through acknowledgment rather than demonstrated through judgment exercised in practice.

This logic becomes especially visible when institutions are found, by regulators or legislative bodies, to have acted improperly at the executive or organizational level. A common element of corrective action is the expansion or reinforcement of employee training. Such measures are widely accepted — by corporations and oversight bodies alike — as legitimate responses.

Yet the implication is subtle and consequential. Even when failures originate at the highest levels of authority, remediation is directed downward. The broader body of employees is retrained, re-certified, and re-aligned, as though the deficiency were collective rather than concentrated. Responsibility is redistributed not through accountability, but through instruction.

What is corrected, in effect, is not decision-making power but behavioral alignment. Training absorbs fault without naming it. The organization adjusts itself by internalizing error across the whole, reinforcing the sense that compliance is never complete and vigilance must never lapse.

Responsibility thus becomes both diffuse and personal. Authority avoids decisive judgment in favor of procedural maintenance, while the burden of conformity rests permanently on the individual. The employee is not declared trustworthy and released; he remains subject to continual demonstration.

This is not an accident of scale. It is **a structural feature of** systems that privilege **defensibility over discretion** and **process over closure**.

CERTIFICATION, RENEWAL, AND THE MANAGED PROFESSIONAL

The architecture described thus far is not confined to large organizations. It extends beyond them into professions once understood as self-governing and character-based. Physicians, therapists, attorneys, engineers, educators, and licensed trades increasingly operate under regimes of continuing education, periodic recertification, and mandatory training imposed by professional boards, associations, or public authorities.

Implicit in earlier systems of credentialing was a presumption of competence. Certification marked not only the attainment of skill, but the judgment that the individual was capable of sustaining that competence through continued engagement with the practice itself. Learning did not end, but it was assumed to occur internally — through experience, responsibility, and the demands of real work.

Ongoing qualification was therefore tacit rather than procedural. Renewal signified standing, not supervision. Oversight existed, but it was episodic, triggered by failure rather than assumed by default. The physician was trusted to remain a physician; the attorney, to remain an attorney.

The contemporary model reverses this presumption. Competence is no longer assumed to persist; it must be continually demonstrated through external processes. Qualification is no longer something one maintains through practice, but something one repeatedly proves through participation. Trust is displaced by verification.

What changes is not the expectation of learning, but its ownership. Responsibility for professional development shifts outward, even as it is executed inwardly through mandated participation. Judgment is replaced by attestation. The professional remains qualified only insofar as he remains aligned with evolving procedural requirements. Standing is not held; it is renewed.

Here again, the stated purpose is practical. Ongoing training ensures competence. Renewal protects the public. Standards must evolve. Few would dispute the necessity of maintaining professional knowledge in a changing world.

Yet the form this maintenance has taken reveals the same logic already observed. Credentials expire. Permissions must be reaffirmed. Much of what is required bears only indirect relation to the practitioner's actual work, focusing instead on compliance, reporting obligations, and approved frameworks of conduct. Ethical standing is demonstrated not through judgment exercised in difficult cases, but through completion and acknowledgment.

What emerges is a form of regulation that does not simply govern institutions, but inhabits the individual. Even outside corporate structures, the professional remains subject to continuous adjustment. **Permission to practice is never final**. It is renewed, monitored, and conditional.

LICENSED USE AND THE LOGIC OF PERMISSION

The following interlude steps briefly outside the historical narrative to show the same architecture at work in a domain largely untouched by ideology, morality, crisis, or political controversy.

Consider the computer software industry. Where users once purchased programs outright — licensed for a fixed number of devices or users — most contemporary software now operates through continuous authentication. Access is granted not by possession, but by ongoing verification. One signs in. One remains signed in. Use is permitted so long as conditions are met.

What emerges is a relationship **no longer defined by ownership, but by permission**. The user exists within an external system that remains aware of status, authorization, and compliance. Access is not assumed; it is maintained.

The stated reasons for this shift are practical and familiar. Software must be updated. Security must be maintained. Support must be funded. Few would dispute the legitimacy of these concerns. Yet the form this solution has taken mirrors the logic already observed elsewhere.

Use is no longer something acquired and held. It is provisioned. Licenses expire. Subscriptions renew. Access may be modified, restricted, or withdrawn. Authorization must be continually reaffirmed.

What changes is not the necessity of maintenance, but the structure of the relationship. Completion disappears. There is no moment at which one is simply *done*. The user remains conditionally permitted and continuously adjustable.

This example is not moral, juridical, or therapeutic. It is technical. Precisely for that reason, it reveals the underlying architecture with particular clarity: permission over possession, renewal over standing, access without finality.

The pattern is not generated by ethics, law, or crisis response, but emerges from the practical requirements of long-term system management. In software, this logic appears in its most stripped-down form. When applied to human life, it fits neatly into the ongoing provisional existence of the manufactured man.

RELIABILITY, REPLACEMENT, AND THE VANISHING END-STATE

The same logic appears in the design and consumption of everyday goods, the trend having been commented on by consumers for decades. For much of the industrial age, reliability and repairability were central virtues of manufactured objects. Products were expected to endure. When they failed, they were serviced. Maintenance was part of ownership, and longevity was a measure of quality.

This orientation has gradually shifted. Many contemporary products are designed less for durability than for replacement. Devices are sealed rather than serviceable. Repair is discouraged, impractical, or economically irrational. Functional obsolescence often arrives alongside physical failure, as advancing technology renders older models outdated even before they cease to operate.

The reasons for this shift are largely pragmatic. Innovation cycles are faster. Performance improves rapidly. Consumer expectations change. Few would deny the genuine advantages this has produced.

Yet the structural consequence is worth noting. Objects are no longer meant to be sustained through care; they are meant to be **replaced through upgrade**. The relationship between user and product becomes temporary by design. There is no expectation of completion, only succession.

What disappears is not quality, but finality. Ownership no longer culminates in stewardship; it remains provisional. The user does not finish with the object — there is no moment of completion; he simply moves on to its replacement. The system rarely asks for maintenance of an item, only for renewal.

Here again, the pattern is not moral, juridical, or therapeutic. It is functional. Precisely for that reason, it reveals the same underlying architecture in our lives: continuity without conclusion, replacement without restoration, use without a terminal state.

Risk, Exposure, and the Permanently Probationary Subject

The same reversal of presumption appears most starkly where authority once acted with greatest finality. Criminal justice was historically organized around discrete judgment and closure. A sentence was imposed, served, and completed. Punishment, however severe, had a terminus. Once paid, the debt was understood — at least in principle — to be discharged.

That logic has shifted.

In many contemporary systems, criminal sanction no longer centers on confinement alone, nor even primarily on it. Increasingly, it unfolds through extended supervision: diversion programs, suspended privileges, registries, electronic monitoring, mandated counseling, compliance checks, and long-term probationary conditions. The language is again therapeutic. These measures are presented as alternatives to punishment, as humane refinements, as instruments of rehabilitation and public safety.

Structurally, however, they operate in a different register. They do not conclude so much as persist.

The individual subject to such regimes is not simply punished and released; he is managed. Obligations are ongoing. Conditions are revisable. Violations need not involve new wrongdoing; failure to comply with procedural requirements may suffice. Oversight becomes ambient rather than episodic.

Here, too, the presumption is reversed. The subject is no longer trusted to resume ordinary standing once a sentence is served. Risk is assumed to remain. Supervision is extended not because of demonstrated failure, but because completion itself is no longer decisive. Freedom becomes conditional, and the conditions are continuous.

What matters most is not the gravity of the original offense, but the capacity for alignment. The individual must demonstrate responsiveness to guidance, adherence to evolving requirements, and willingness to remain visible. The sentence does not end; it is administered.

This model mirrors the logic already observed in corporate training, professional certification, and licensed access. Responsibility is redistributed downward. Authority avoids decisive judgment in favor of procedural maintenance. The burden of proof shifts permanently onto the individual, who must continually show that he remains fit to be left alone.

The resulting condition is best described not as punishment, but as probationary existence. One is not declared restored; one is permitted to continue. Standing is provisional. Oversight becomes a background feature of life rather than an exceptional intervention.

Once again, this is not a claim about intention. It is an observation about structure. Systems organized around risk minimization favor persistence over closure. They do not aim to form character or restore trust; they aim to manage exposure. The subject is **not corrected and released, but retained within a framework of ongoing adjustment.**

The sentence, here as elsewhere, is no longer finished.

PUBLIC HEALTH AS PROCESS

The same architecture becomes fully visible when it is activated under conditions of emergency. Public health provides a particularly clear illustration — not because it is unique, but because it gathers, in compressed form, mechanisms that now operate separately in everyday institutional life.

Historically, public health responses to disease were organized as discrete campaigns. Smallpox, polio, measles, and other widespread illnesses were addressed through finite interventions: vaccination drives, public advisories, localized restrictions, and eventual resolution. Measures varied in severity and success, but their structure was broadly consistent. An intervention was announced, implemented, and concluded. The public health emergency had an end-state.

Even the influenza pandemic of 1918, severe as it was, followed this pattern. Authorities issued warnings, limited gatherings, and encouraged protective measures. Enforcement was uneven and often local. Responsibility rested primarily with institutions and community leaders. But when the crisis passed, extraordinary measures receded.

The contemporary response to COVID unfolded differently.

From the outset, authority was exercised primarily through guidance rather than command. Recommendations were issued continuously, revised frequently, and disseminated across multiple levels: federal agencies, state authorities, local governments, institutions, and media. Guidance moved rapidly from advisory statements to expectations of conduct, often without a clear moment of transition.

What was communicated most consistently was not rationale, but instruction. The emphasis fell on *what* actions were required rather than *why* particular measures were judged necessary in specific contexts. Explanation receded as alignment took its place. Compliance became the visible marker of responsibility.

Dissemination was ubiquitous. Guidance appeared on news broadcasts, institutional signage, retail environments, social media platforms, and workplace communications. It accompanied ordinary activity — entering a store, sitting at a table, attending a meeting. Enforcement did not rely primarily on direct sanction. Instead, it was widely distributed and socially mediated.

Peer pressure performed much of the regulatory work. Individuals monitored one another's behavior, corrected deviations, and signaled alignment publicly. Non-compliance carried reputational cost. Many found themselves engaged in continuous self-assessment, uncertain whether their actions met evolving expectations. Suspicion — often unspoken — became ambient.

Public health thus shifted from a series of interventions to an ongoing process. Metrics replaced milestones. Thresholds were introduced, adjusted, and recalibrated. Permissions expanded and contracted. Activities were conditionally allowed, withdrawn, and reinstated under modified terms. There was no single moment of completion. Management persisted.

Participation remained mandatory, but the tone was therapeutic. Individuals were urged to act responsibly, to remain attentive, to adapt continuously. The burden of interpretation shifted downward. One was expected not merely to comply with explicit rules, but to anticipate them — to remain aligned even in advance of formal instruction.

What distinguished this moment was not the severity of the disease alone, but the form of governance it revealed. Public health authority now operated through continuous adjustment rather than discrete judgment. Responsibility was internalized. The individual was enlisted as the manager of his own risk profile, accountable not only to institutions, but to peers and to himself.

This account offers no judgment on the necessity, wisdom, or effectiveness of particular measures. Emergencies demand response, and public health must act under uncertainty. The point here is structural, not moral. What COVID revealed was not a temporary departure from normal governance, but the activation — under pressure — of an architecture already present in everyday institutional life.

Guidance replaced command. Process replaced closure. Alignment replaced judgment.

The emergency did not end so much as recede into maintenance.

RECOGNITION WITHOUT RESOLUTION

By this point, a pattern should be visible — not as an argument to be accepted, but as a condition to be recognized. Across domains that differ in purpose, scale, and moral weight, the same architecture has appeared with remarkable consistency. Corporate life, professional standing, licensed access, everyday consumption, public sanction, and emergency response have come to operate through guidance rather than command, renewal rather than completion, and alignment rather than judgment.

What unites these domains is not ideology, nor a shared intention. It is function. Systems designed to manage risk, complexity, and uncertainty favor continuity over closure. They **replace decisive judgment with ongoing adjustment**. Responsibility is redistributed downward, internalized, and maintained through visibility, participation, and self-regulation.

Unlike the classical concept of tyranny, authority no longer needs to declare itself as force. It does not primarily act upon bodies, seize property, or impose final sentences. Instead, it organizes conditions under which individuals learn to manage themselves — anticipating expectations, avoiding exposure, and remaining provisionally aligned.

In this environment, standing is rarely settled. Credentials expire. Access must be renewed. Compliance is never complete. The sentence does not end; it is administered. The individual is not restored and released, but retained within a framework of continual adjustment.

This condition produces neither villains nor heroes. It does not depend on bad faith or conspiracy. It emerges from systems that seek to function smoothly under perpetual revision. Yet it carries consequences nonetheless. When closure disappears, so does relief. When judgment is replaced by procedure, character recedes from view. What remains is a form of life defined by maintenance rather than resolution.

This chapter has not sought to explain how we arrived here, nor to propose what should be done. It has sought only to make the present condition visible, without consolation or conclusion. It has aimed only to make the present condition intelligible. Across the long arc traced in this book — from inherited forms of meaning, through the revolutions of thought and method, into the therapeutic and algorithmic structures of modern life — the manufactured man has emerged not as a figure imposed by force, but as a condition sustained by systems of continuous adjustment. He is not primarily coerced. He is managed. He participates. He adjusts. He remains.

What follows will not ask again how this apparatus operates. That work is complete. It will ask a different question — one that has been implicit throughout, but never yet confronted directly: where are the limits of engineering, and what happens when they are reached?

Part VI:
The Limits of Engineering

Chapter 20
The Unmakeable Human

Engineering succeeds best where the material yields predictably to method. Steel can be stressed, software updated, processes optimized, and behavior guided within defined parameters. The difficulty begins when these assumptions are extended to the human being himself.

For all the sophistication of modern systems, the human person remains only partially amenable to management. He can be guided, nudged, monitored, and aligned — but not fully determined. Certain capacities resist procedural capture: judgment under uncertainty, meaning forged through suffering, loyalty that is not incentivized, and conscience that does not resolve into compliance. These are not defects of design. They are resilient features of the human condition.

This chapter examines those limits — not as ideals to be reclaimed, but as realities that persist regardless of intention. Where engineering reaches beyond them, something does not merely fail; something distorts. The question is no longer how systems operate, but what they cannot absorb without breaking.

JUDGMENT CANNOT BE AUTOMATED

Modern systems excel at rule application. They can process vast quantities of information, identify patterns, and enforce consistency at scale. This is their strength. Yet judgment is not the same as rule-following, and no amount of procedural refinement can make it so.

Judgment arises precisely where rules run out. It operates under uncertainty, incomplete information, and competing goods. It requires discernment rather than compliance. When systems attempt to replace judgment with procedure, they do not eliminate error; they relocate it. The individual is no longer asked to decide rightly, but to select the correct protocol.

The consequence is not clarity, but brittleness. Situations that fall outside predefined categories are mishandled, escalated, or ignored. Responsibility becomes ambiguous. When outcomes are poor, blame attaches not to decision-makers but to process deviations.

In such environments, discretion is treated as risk rather than competence. The human capacity to judge becomes something to be constrained, audited, or bypassed. Yet the need for judgment does not disappear. It re-emerges at the margins, where systems fail most visibly.

Engineering can optimize for consistency. It cannot replace wisdom.

MEANING CANNOT BE ASSIGNED

Systems can shape behavior, but they cannot confer meaning. Meaning is not delivered through instruction or produced through alignment. It arises through experience, commitment, sacrifice, and choice. It is discovered, not imposed.

The modern apparatus increasingly treats meaning as a variable to be managed. Values are articulated, missions declared, narratives curated. Individuals are invited to identify with these frameworks, to internalize them, to see themselves reflected within institutional language.

Yet meaning does not behave like data. It cannot be standardized without dilution. When meaning is supplied externally, it becomes thin, interchangeable, and fragile. Individuals may comply, perform, or signal agreement — but inwardly, significance recedes.

What follows is not nihilism, but exhaustion. When systems promise purpose but deliver procedure, the result is not rebellion but disengagement. Meaning retreats into private life or collapses into irony.

Engineering can manage outcomes. It cannot generate purpose.

LOYALTY CANNOT BE INCENTIVIZED

Incentives are powerful tools. They can direct attention, shape behavior, and reinforce compliance. But loyalty is not a function of incentive, and when treated as such, it dissolves.

Loyalty presupposes trust, mutual obligation, and continuity. It involves standing with something even when advantage is uncertain. Incentive structures, by contrast, are transactional. They reward performance, not commitment. They assume rational calculation rather than allegiance.

When systems attempt to engineer loyalty through incentives, they produce only alignment. Alignment persists so long as conditions are favorable. When circumstances change, it evaporates. What remains is not betrayal, but indifference.

The attempt to manage loyalty procedurally replaces bonds with metrics and belonging with participation. Individuals remain compliant, but attachment thins. The system gains predictability at the cost of devotion.

Engineering can secure cooperation. It cannot produce fidelity.

CONSCIENCE CANNOT BE PROCEDURALIZED

Conscience is not a rule set. It does not emerge from compliance training or policy acknowledgment. It interrupts. It resists. It introduces friction precisely where systems seek smooth operation.

Modern governance often treats conscience as a failure mode. Non-compliance is pathologized. Dissent is reframed as misunderstanding. Moral refusal is managed through escalation rather than engagement.

Yet conscience does not disappear when suppressed. It reappears as withdrawal, burnout, moral injury, or sudden rupture. The individual may continue to function, but inwardly disengages. The system retains order, but loses legitimacy.

Where conscience is replaced by procedure, moral responsibility is displaced. The individual is no longer asked what is right, only whether requirements have been met. Ethical life collapses into rule adherence.

Engineering can enforce conformity. It cannot silence conscience without cost.

BIOLOGY, CULTURE, AND THE RETURN OF LIMITS

When engineering exceeds its proper domain, the result is not total control, but distortion. **Systems become rigid where flexibility is needed and permissive where judgment is required**. Individuals adapt outwardly while disengaging inwardly.

The problem is not that systems seek order, but that they mistake order for sufficiency. They assume that with sufficient refinement, friction can be eliminated. Yet friction is not a flaw; it is a signal of irreducibility.

Where limits are denied, they return as crisis. Where judgment is suppressed, error multiplies. Where meaning is prescribed, emptiness spreads. The cost is not immediately visible, but it accumulates.

Engineering does not fail because it is malicious. It fails because it encounters what it cannot absorb.

WHAT REMAINS

What remains after engineering reaches its limit is not chaos, but the human being himself — unfinished, unoptimized, and irreducible. Judgment under uncertainty. Meaning discovered rather than assigned. Loyalty that cannot be bought. Conscience that interrupts.

These capacities persist not because systems allow them, but because they cannot be removed without loss. They are not obstacles to be overcome, but realities to be acknowledged.

The question is no longer whether engineering will continue. It will. The question is whether any given system recognizes its limits before distortion overtakes function.

That question leads not to rejection, but to proportion.

Chapter 21
Civilizational Resistance: the Non-Enlightenment Polities

The doctrine of human makeability — the belief that man can be redesigned through rational method, institutional arrangement, and procedural correction — did not spread evenly across civilizations. While it reshaped much of Western Europe and its cultural descendants, other societies absorbed it only partially, selectively, or not at all. This divergence is not a matter of intelligence or development. It is a matter of metaphysical orientation.

Some civilizations never accepted the Enlightenment premise that human nature is fundamentally plastic. Where the Enlightenment desacralized man and society, these cultures retained an understanding of human life as bounded — by fate, by divine order, by inherited law, or by metaphysical necessity. As a result, attempts at comprehensive human engineering encountered resistance not merely at the political level, but at the level of meaning.

This chapter examines two broad cases — Russia and the Islamic world — not as alternatives to be adopted or rejected, but as civilizational counterbalances that complicate the narrative traced thus far. Their structures limited the penetration of the makeability doctrine in ways that illuminate its contingency. Their resistance is neither absolute nor without cost, but it serves to re-situate the argument within a world that is not monolithic.

Russia: Fatalism, Orthodoxy, and the Limits of Rational Redesign

Russian civilization absorbed elements of Enlightenment rationalism unevenly and often under compulsion. Westernizing reforms — from Peter the Great through Soviet industrialization — were imposed from above, frequently in defiance of deeply rooted cultural assumptions. The result was not synthesis, but oscillation.

At the core of Russian metaphysics lies a fatalistic orientation toward history and suffering. Eastern Orthodox Christianity emphasizes endurance, sacrifice, and the redemptive meaning of suffering rather than mastery over conditions. Human life is understood less as a project to be optimized than as a trial to be borne. Salvation is not achieved through system design, but through humility, repentance, and endurance.

This orientation produced a population capable of surviving extreme hardship without internalizing the Enlightenment belief that suffering indicates systemic failure. Where Western systems seek to eliminate friction, Russian culture has often absorbed it as unavoidable. The expectation that life should be made comfortable, rational, or fully coherent never took deep root.

As a result, Russian society has shown limited receptivity to therapeutic governance. Psychological optimization, moral management, and procedural self-correction never became dominant modes of legitimacy. Authority remained external, personal, and often brutal — but rarely internalized as a project of self-improvement.

The Soviet experiment represents a partial exception. Marxist-Leninism imported Enlightenment assumptions about human plasticity and attempted to engineer the "New Soviet Man." Yet this project never fully displaced older metaphysical structures. The result was not the manufactured man of the West, but a dual existence: outward conformity paired with inward detachment. The system demanded performance, not belief.

When the Soviet apparatus collapsed, what re-emerged was not liberal makeability, but older patterns: centralized authority, cultural fatalism, and suspicion toward rational redesign. Russian resistance to Enlightenment engineering was not ideological. It was existential.

ISLAM: DIVINE LAW AND THE NON-NEGOTIABILITY OF HUMAN NATURE

Islamic civilization represents a different form of resistance. Where the Enlightenment replaced divine law with human reason, Islam retained a comprehensive metaphysical framework in which law, morality, and social order are grounded in revelation rather than rational construction.

In Islamic thought, human nature is not infinitely malleable. It is fallen, constrained, and oriented toward obedience to divine command. The task of society is not to redesign the human being, but to align conduct with an already given moral order. Sharia is not a system of improvement, but of submission.

This metaphysical foundation sharply limits the appeal of Enlightenment makeability. Attempts to introduce therapeutic governance, psychological optimization, or moral self-engineering often encounter resistance — not because they are ineffective, but because they conflict with non-negotiable assumptions about authority and meaning.

Where Western systems internalize control, Islamic societies tend to externalize it. Moral authority resides in law, tradition, and communal enforcement rather than individual self-regulation. Conscience is oriented upward, not inward. The self is not a project; it is a servant.

Modernization efforts within Islamic societies have therefore produced tension rather than transformation. Secular institutions may be adopted, but they coexist uneasily with older metaphysical commitments. The result is fragmentation rather than synthesis.

This resistance is not without cost, nor should it be misunderstood. Islamic civilizations have not been hostile to science, technology, or administrative modernization. On the contrary, earlier Islamic societies preserved and advanced scientific knowledge during periods when much of Europe did not, and contemporary states such as Saudi Arabia, Qatar, and the United Arab Emirates demonstrate rapid technological and infrastructural adaptation.

What has been resisted more consistently is not modernity itself, but the Enlightenment doctrine of human makeability — the belief that moral character, identity, and purpose can be redesigned through rational procedure and therapeutic management. Scientific and technical systems may be adopted readily, but the inward re-engineering of the self encounters firmer metaphysical limits.

As a result, modernization often proceeds without the internalization of therapeutic governance that characterizes the manufactured man. Authority remains external, moral order remains given, and meaning is not treated as a variable to be optimized.

RESISTANCE IS NOT IMMUNITY

Civilizational resistance to makeability should not be romanticized. Russia and the Islamic world have experienced authoritarianism, stagnation, violence, and repression. Externalized authority can be cruel. Fatalism can become resignation. Divine law can harden into coercion.

The point is not that resistance produces better societies, but that it produces *different* **failure modes.**

Where Enlightenment cultures suffer from internalized control and loss of meaning, non-Enlightenment polities often suffer from rigidity and suppression. Neither path is cost-free. Both confront limits.

What matters is the contrast. Western societies attempted to abolish limits through engineering. These civilizations preserved limits by rejecting the premise of makeability itself.

WHAT RESISTANCE REVEALS

The existence of civilizational resistance demonstrates that the manufactured man is not inevitable. He is contingent. He emerges where specific metaphysical assumptions take hold: that human nature is plastic, that suffering indicates failure, that meaning can be assigned, and that systems can replace judgment.

Where these assumptions are absent or contested, engineering encounters friction earlier and more visibly. Control remains external. Identity remains inherited. Meaning remains anchored beyond the system.

This does not resolve the crisis of meaning explored in Part V. But it clarifies its origin. The crisis is not universal. It is civilizational.

THE LIMITS REASSERTED

Across all societies, limits eventually reassert themselves. Where they are denied, they return as distortion. Where they are acknowledged, they constrain ambition.

Civilizational resistance is one way that limits survive. It is not the only way, nor necessarily the best. But it reveals that the Enlightenment's project of universal makeability was never universally accepted — and that human nature cannot be fully redesigned without cost.

Here we have examined two traditions, but others — shaped by different metaphysical assumptions — have likewise retained limits on human plasticity, reminding us that **the path traced in this book is neither universal nor inevitable**. Religions oriented toward harmony rather than mastery, submission rather than optimization, or grace rather than technique — Buddhism, Hinduism, and forms of Christianity among them — have often resisted the reduction of the self to an object of continual redesign, even when they have adopted modern institutions and technologies.

The point is not to catalogue exceptions, but to reestablish proportion. The world is not monolithic, and the path traced in this book is not inevitable. The persistence of limits across cultures suggests that what resists engineering is not a defect of development, but a property of being human.

The question now is not which civilization was right, but what can be learned from the persistence of those limits.

That question brings us to the final reckoning of the limits of engineering: the cost of perfectibility.

The stakes of this resistance are not merely theoretical. In societies where loyalty, propriety, and dignity are organized as external and relational goods — anchored in family, status, honor, and public conduct — efforts to internalize control through therapeutic or psychological frameworks often prove corrosive rather than corrective. A familiar example appears in commercial life — the handshake versus the contract. In many honor-based societies, trust is sustained through reputation, family standing, and public accountability rather than through dense contractual enforcement. When Western compliance frameworks are imposed wholesale — replacing external honor with internalized procedural obligation — transactions may become legally safer yet socially thinner, and trust itself often degrades rather than deepens.

What Western systems seek to manage inwardly may, in these contexts, be sustained only through outward recognition and shared norms. Certain social and moral goods do not reside primarily within the individual; they are maintained publicly, relationally, and through visible obligation.

When such goods are reframed psychologically — as matters of personal adjustment or moral self-optimization — they do not gradually reform. They fracture, or lose their governing force altogether.

Chapter 22
The Cost of Perfectibility

The pursuit of perfectibility has always been animated by good intentions. Few projects of human redesign began with malice. They emerged from a belief that suffering is unnecessary, that error can be corrected, and that rational intervention can improve the human condition. These assumptions were not unreasonable. They were, in many cases, humane.

Yet intentions do not determine outcomes.

When perfectibility becomes an organizing principle rather than an aspiration, costs begin to accumulate — sometimes inconspicuously at first, then persistently. The problem is not that improvement is sought, but that it is treated as unbounded. Systems designed to reduce harm are extended beyond their proper domain. What cannot be resolved is managed. What cannot be finished is optimized. The result is not perfection, but strain.

This chapter examines those costs — not as moral failures, but as structural consequences of the engineering impulse when it exceeds its limits.

THE FAILURE OF UTOPIAS

Utopian projects fail not because they aim too high, but because they misunderstand what can be made. They assume that human nature is sufficiently plastic to conform to rational design, and that resistance indicates error rather than irreducibility.

History provides abundant examples — revolutionary states, planned communities, technocratic reforms, moral purification movements, and educational or therapeutic experiments organized around idealized conceptions of the human being. Such projects rarely collapse through immediate repression. They erode through mismatch. Behavior conforms outwardly while disengaging inwardly. Participation persists; belief does not.

When outcomes fall short, the response is rarely reconsideration of premise. It is refinement of method. Rules are clarified. Incentives are adjusted. Deviations are explained as misunderstanding or bad faith. The system doubles down.

The cost is not tyranny alone, but brittleness. Utopias cannot tolerate ambiguity. They cannot absorb contradiction. They fail where judgment is required and conscience intrudes. Eventually, the ever-increasing **distance between design and reality** becomes unsustainable.

Utopias do not end in perfection. They end in management.

OPTIMIZATION AND ITS SHADOW

Optimization is among the great achievements of modern engineering. It reduces waste, increases efficiency, and improves performance across domains. Applied appropriately, it delivers undeniable benefit. Applied indiscriminately, it produces shadow effects.

When systems optimize for measurable outcomes, they privilege what can be counted over what can be known. *What gets measured gets done.* Metrics displace meaning. Targets replace judgment. The appearance of improvement masks the loss of context.

In human systems, optimization often erodes precisely those qualities it cannot measure: trust, loyalty, courage, discretion. These are not eliminated deliberately. They are crowded out. What remains is compliance without commitment and performance without belief.

The shadow of optimization is not failure, but narrowing. As systems become more efficient, they become less humane. They succeed at scale while faltering at edges. Exceptional cases proliferate. Moral injury accumulates.

Optimization does not destroy values. It renders them irrelevant.

THE EXHAUSTION OF IMPROVEMENT

A less visible cost of perfectibility is exhaustion. When improvement is treated as continuous and obligatory, rest becomes suspect. Completion disappears. The individual is never finished, never sufficient, never complete.

This exhaustion is not physical alone. It is existential.

In a system oriented toward perpetual enhancement, the self becomes a project without end. Skills must be updated. Attitudes adjusted. Awareness refined. Alignment maintained. The promise of improvement becomes a demand.

What begins as opportunity hardens into obligation. The individual internalizes the imperative to improve, even in the absence of failure. Fatigue is interpreted as resistance. Doubt becomes deficiency.

The result is not progress, but wear. One's **foundation that supports everyday life weakens**. Improvement loses its meaning when it has no point of completion. The cost is not collapse, but progressive depletion.

Perfectibility, pursued without limit, consumes what it seeks to refine.

MORAL INJURY AND PROCEDURAL GUILT

As systems expand, moral responsibility is increasingly displaced by procedure. Individuals are asked not to judge rightly, but to comply correctly. When harm occurs, responsibility becomes diffuse. No one decides; the system proceeds.

Yet conscience does not disappear. It registers the **gap between action and meaning**.

This produces a distinctive form of moral injury. Individuals experience guilt without agency and responsibility without judgment. They follow rules that conflict with intuition, execute procedures that feel misaligned, and participate in outcomes they did not choose.

Because the system is functioning as designed, dissent appears irrational. Objection becomes non-compliance. The individual is left to carry moral burden without moral authority.

Procedural guilt accumulates not through wrongdoing, but through participation.

THE LOSS OF PROPORTION

The deepest cost of perfectibility is the loss of proportion.

Classical ethics understood limits not as constraints to be overcome, but as conditions of flourishing. Excess and deficiency were equally destructive. Wisdom lay in measure.

The engineering impulse reverses this orientation. Limits are treated as problems. Friction is seen as inefficiency. Suffering signals failure. The idea that some things should not be optimized becomes unintelligible.

As proportion disappears, so does restraint. Systems pursue improvement where acceptance is required, control where trust is necessary, and correction where understanding would suffice.

The result is **not greater humanity, but distortion**. What cannot be improved is pressured until it breaks.

THE COST MADE VISIBLE

The cost of perfectibility is not always dramatic. It does not announce itself as catastrophe. More often, it appears as declining trust, moral fatigue, procedural overload, disengagement masked as participation, or systems that function without conviction

These **costs are cumulative**. They are easy to dismiss individually. Together, they alter the texture of life.

Perfectibility promises relief from suffering. Without limits, it produces a different kind of suffering — subtle, more persistent, and harder to name.

WHAT THE COST TEACHES

The cost of perfectibility does not invalidate engineering. It clarifies its domain.

Engineering excels at what can be designed, optimized, and controlled. It fails where judgment, meaning, loyalty, and conscience are required. The lesson is not rejection, but proportion.

Where limits are acknowledged, systems stabilize. Where they are denied, costs escalate. The choice is not between progress and restraint, but between improvement governed by proportion and improvement driven by endless correction.

The price of ignoring limits is not failure alone. It is erosion.

Part VII:
Beyond the Manufactured
Man

Chapter 23
The Recovery of Limits

The recovery of limits does not begin with rejection. It begins with recognition. Having traced how the belief in human makeability emerged, expanded, and encountered its constraints, the task now is not to dismantle systems nor to escape modernity, but to reorient our posture within it.

Limits, in this sense, are not obstacles to be overcome. They are conditions to be inhabited.

Pre-modern societies did not experience limits primarily as frustration. They experienced them as givens — features of reality that shaped judgment, expectation, and meaning. Human life was understood to be bounded by nature, by time, by mortality, by inheritance, and by circumstance. Within those bounds, dignity was not diminished. It was made possible.

Modernity inverted this relationship. Limits came to be treated as problems. Friction signaled inefficiency. Imperfection implied failure. What could not be optimized appeared suspect. In seeking to free humanity from constraint, modern systems inadvertently stripped constraint of its human meaning.

This chapter does not propose a return to pre-modern life. The conditions that sustained earlier forms of meaning cannot simply be recreated. Nor would that be desirable. What can be recovered, however, is a way of seeing: an understanding that not everything valuable can be planned, not everything meaningful can be improved, and not everything human should be managed.

The recovery of limits is therefore not a technical project. It is an ethical and existential one. It concerns how we live with uncertainty, how we accept finitude, and how we locate dignity in what resists design. It asks not how to perfect the human being, but how to stand rightly within the conditions of being human.

Beyond the manufactured man lies not a solution, but a stance — to **accept limits without resignation** and **inhabit imperfection without shame**.

LIMITS AS ORIENTATION, NOT FAILURE

Modern life trains us to interpret limits as defects. Friction implies inefficiency. Delay suggests mismanagement. Constraint appears as a problem to be solved. Within this frame, the absence of limit becomes the measure of progress, and the capacity to overcome constraint becomes the measure of intelligence.

This assumption is neither ancient nor universal. For most of human history, limits were not experienced primarily as failure. They were experienced as *orientation*. Boundaries did not merely restrict action; they gave it shape. To know what could not be done was to know where judgment was required. To accept finitude was to locate responsibility.

Earlier societies inhabited limits differently. Travel took days or weeks, and this was not experienced as wasted time awaiting resolution. John Adams, crossing long distances on horseback, read while in the saddle, allowing the horse to manage the journey while the interval was filled with thought. "You will never be alone," he wrote to his son, "with a poet in your pocket."[50] Delay was not an interruption of life, but part of its texture.

Such limits did not merely slow action; they oriented it. Time was not something to be eliminated, but something to be occupied. Constraint created interior space, and waiting did not demand justification.

---

[50] Letter from John Adams to his son, John Quincy Adams, May 14, 1781.

Pre-modern wisdom traditions understood that action without boundary is not freedom, but confusion. Limits clarified roles, obligations, and expectations. They distinguished ambition from hubris and courage from recklessness. Human excellence was not defined by boundlessness, but by measure.

The Enlightenment's reconfiguration of limits altered this relationship. Once limits were understood as contingent rather than given, they became negotiable. Once negotiable, they became suspect. The task of reason shifted from discerning where limits lay to determining how they might be surpassed. What had once guided judgment now provoked correction.

The consequence was not merely technological advance, but a change in moral posture. Where limits had oriented action, they now interrupted it. Where boundaries had stabilized meaning, they now signaled inefficiency. The question ceased to be *What is fitting here?* and became *How can this be improved?*

Orientation requires constraint. Without limits, judgment loses its bearings. Choice proliferates without guidance. Responsibility diffuses. The freedom to act becomes the burden to decide without measure. What appears as liberation often produces anxiety rather than agency.

Limits function differently than prohibitions. A prohibition says *do not*. **A limit says *here***. It marks a terrain rather than an interdiction. Within that terrain, creativity, responsibility, and dignity can emerge. Beyond it, action becomes unmoored.

To recover limits, then, is not to retreat from modern life, but to recover proportion within it. It is to recognize that not every boundary is an obstacle, and not every constraint a failure. **Some limits exist not to be overcome, but to be inhabited**.

This recovery does not require abandoning engineering, systems, or progress. It requires remembering that orientation precedes optimization. Before asking how far we can go, we must know where we stand.

That knowledge does not arrive through design. It arrives through recognition.

IMPERFECTION AS DIGNITY

The modern imagination associates dignity with flawlessness. Error appears as deficiency. Incompleteness suggests inadequacy. Improvement becomes the moral imperative by which worth is measured. Within this frame, to be imperfect is to be unfinished, and to be unfinished is to be insufficient.

Pre-modern understandings of dignity were different. **Human worth did not arise from completion or optimization, but from standing rightly within constraint**. Mortality, limitation, and vulnerability were not embarrassments to be concealed; they were the shared conditions that made responsibility, mercy, and loyalty meaningful.

Imperfection was not merely tolerated. It was assumed — and with it, the necessity of judgment.

A familiar example can clarify what is meant by limits as orientation. In recent decades, childhood itself has increasingly become a site of optimization. Development is measured, tracked, and managed. Time is structured, progress assessed, risks minimized. Play is guided. Emotion is monitored. The child is treated, often with the best of intentions, as a project to be refined.

None of this arises from neglect. It arises from care.

Yet when the impulse to improve crosses a certain threshold, something subtle changes. Unstructured time disappears. Failure is preempted rather than endured. Judgment is replaced by supervision. The child becomes safer, but also more fragile. Confidence gives way to anxiety. Resilience is postponed.

What has been exceeded here is not a rule, but a limit. Childhood requires exposure to uncertainty, boredom, manageable risk, and unplanned encounter. These are not inefficiencies to be eliminated; they are conditions of growth. When they are removed in the name of optimization, development does not accelerate. It distorts.

This is not a condemnation of guidance or care. It is an illustration of what happens when a system designed to help forgets what cannot be supplied by design.

The attempt to remove imperfection through design misunderstands its role. Error is not simply noise in the system; it is often the site where judgment is formed. Failure teaches proportion. Mistakes invite repair, and repair invites relationship. **A world without error would not be a world without harm; it would be a world without forgiveness**.

When systems pursue flawlessness, they often erode the very dignity they seek to preserve. Individuals become anxious under constant evaluation. Performance replaces presence. Worth is measured against shifting standards that can never be fully satisfied. What is lost is not excellence, but acceptance.

Dignity does not require perfection. It requires recognition. To be human is to be unfinished, and that unfinishedness is not a problem to be solved. It is the condition within which character is revealed.

Dignity is formed through encounter — through success and failure, gain and loss, affirmation and disappointment. These experiences establish proportion, allowing one to distinguish what matters from what does not, to respond with appropriate weight rather than reflex. A life that has absorbed such contrasts stands more securely, not because it is insulated from harm, but because it has learned where harm belongs.

THE UNPLANNED AS SOURCE OF MEANING

Meaning rarely arrives according to plan. It emerges through encounter, accident, interruption, and loss. Love is not scheduled. Vocation is not optimized. Loyalty is not engineered.

The most consequential moments of a life are often those that resist anticipation.

Modern systems struggle with this reality because they privilege intention over encounter. Purpose is defined in advance. Goals are articulated, milestones set, outcomes measured. What does not fit the plan appears wasteful or inefficient.

Yet meaning does not obey efficiency. It arises when intention yields to circumstance and when control gives way to response. Pre-modern wisdom recognized this implicitly. Fate, providence, and fortune named not passivity, but openness — the recognition that life unfolds beyond human design.

The effort to manage meaning produces thin substitutes. Mission statements replace calling. Narratives are curated rather than lived. Individuals are encouraged to identify with frameworks rather than discover significance through commitment. Meaning becomes portable, interchangeable, and easily withdrawn.

What is lost is depth.

The unplanned does not guarantee meaning, but it makes it possible. **Where life is fully scripted, nothing is at stake. Where everything is optimized, nothing is chosen.** Meaning requires exposure to contingency.

To recover the unplanned is not to reject intention, but to release its claim to mastery. It is to allow life to surprise rather than conform.

LIVING WITH SYSTEMS WITHOUT BECOMING ONE

The recovery of limits does not require withdrawal from modern systems. Few can, and fewer should. Work, technology, institutions, and governance are unavoidable features of contemporary life. The task is not escape, but orientation.

Systems are tools. They become dangers only when mistaken for total environments.

To live well within systems requires maintaining a distinction between participation and absorption. One may comply without internalizing. One may use tools without becoming one. One may follow procedures while reserving judgment.

This posture was once common. Roles were inhabited without consuming identity. Authority was obeyed without being worshiped. Individuals navigated institutions while grounding meaning elsewhere — in family, faith, craft, and place.

The manufactured man collapses this distinction. He is invited to identify fully with systems, to align inwardly as well as outwardly, to make procedure his moral compass. Recovery begins by refusing that invitation — not through rebellion, but through restraint.

This does not announce itself. It appears in limits set, in refusals made without drama, in loyalties maintained outside performance, and in judgments exercised even when no metric rewards them.

Living beyond the manufactured man does not require heroism. It requires proportion.

The Recovery That Remains

The recovery of limits is not a return. It does not restore a lost world, nor does it offer a blueprint for a new one. It restores a stance — a way of standing within modernity without being consumed by it.

Limits orient judgment. Imperfection grounds dignity. The unplanned makes meaning possible. Systems serve life only when they do not define it.

These recoveries do not solve the problems diagnosed earlier in the book. They do not promise relief from suffering or error. They offer something more fundamental: the ability to **inhabit**

constraint without resentment and to **accept finitude without shame**.

Beyond the Manufactured Man lies not freedom from systems, but freedom from the illusion that systems can replace judgment, meaning, and conscience.

What remains is the human being — unfinished, limited, and capable of standing rightly within those limits.

Chapter 24
Living Without Blueprints

Modern systems are built on blueprints. They require plans that can be executed, procedures that can be replicated, and models that promise predictable outcomes. In the presence of complexity, they impose structure. In the absence of certainty, they substitute design. This impulse is not malicious. It is how engineering thinks.

The difficulty begins when this posture is extended to human life.

To live without blueprints does not mean to live without intention, care, or responsibility. It means refusing the assumption that a complete plan for human flourishing can be drawn in advance. It means accepting that the most consequential aspects of life — character, meaning, loyalty, and conscience — do not yield to design without loss.

Pre-modern wisdom did not offer blueprints for the good life. It offered orientation. It provided limits, exemplars, and practices rather than plans. One learned how to stand, not how to optimize. **Judgment mattered more than method**. Proportion mattered more than progress.

This chapter does not propose a return to that world. It asks whether something of that posture can be recovered within the modern one.

LUCIDITY OVER IDEOLOGY

Ideology offers relief from uncertainty. It promises coherence where experience is fractured and certainty where judgment is difficult. Its appeal lies not in cruelty, but in comfort.

If the world can be made to fit a single explanatory frame, one need not remain attentive to its contradictions.

Lucidity offers no such relief.

To live lucidly is **to see without demanding resolution**. It is to accept that some tensions cannot be reconciled, some questions cannot be answered, and some goods cannot be harmonized. This is not resignation. It is fidelity to experience.

A familiar example appears in the way modern individuals consume news and commentary. Ideological frames promise immediate interpretation: who is right, who is wrong, what must be done. Lucidity requires something harder. It asks the reader to remain present with incomplete information, conflicting motives, and unresolved outcomes — to resist the urge to collapse complexity into allegiance.

Living without blueprints begins here. Not with withdrawal from the world, but with the refusal to let explanation replace perception.

CHARACTER OVER DESIGN

Design produces behavior. Character produces action.

Modern systems are excellent at shaping behavior. They reward compliance, discourage deviation, and optimize outcomes within defined parameters. What they cannot do is form character. **Character emerges through choice** under uncertainty, through failure and repair, through responsibility borne without guarantee.

No blueprint can specify how a person should act when rules conflict, when incentives misalign, or when conscience intrudes. These moments cannot be engineered in advance. They reveal who someone has become.

A simple example illustrates the difference. Consider the colleague who follows every procedure flawlessly, without evaluation or choice, yet avoids responsibility when judgment is required, and the colleague who occasionally errs but stands openly by decisions made in good faith. Systems reward the first. Human communities trust the second.

To live without blueprints is to accept that character cannot be optimized. It must be formed — slowly, unevenly, and often invisibly.

PRESENCE OVER OPTIMIZATION

Optimization directs attention toward what comes next. **Presence attends to what is here**.

The culture of improvement trains individuals to live in anticipation. Skills must be updated. Habits refined. Awareness enhanced. Even rest becomes instrumental — something undertaken in order to perform better later. Life is experienced as preparation rather than encounter.

The cost of this posture is subtle but real. What is constantly optimized is rarely inhabited.

A common illustration appears in everyday conversation. Devices are consulted reflexively. Moments are documented rather than lived. Attention fragments as the present is treated as a staging ground for something else. Nothing is wrong, exactly — but something is missing.

Presence does not reject improvement. It resists the idea that value lies always beyond the present moment. To be present is to grant sufficiency to what is already here, even if it is imperfect.

Living without blueprints means allowing *some* moments to remain unproductive, unoptimized, and unredeemed — without treating them as waste.

ACTING WITHOUT GUARANTEES

Blueprints promise outcomes. They reduce risk by specifying steps and predicting results. Human life does not offer such assurances.

To act without guarantees is not recklessness. It is the ordinary condition of moral life. One chooses without knowing outcomes. One commits without certainty of reward. One stands by decisions that cannot be validated by metrics.

This posture has largely disappeared from modern discourse, replaced by frameworks of risk management and outcome prediction. Responsibility becomes conditional. Action is deferred until assurance is obtained.

Yet assurance never fully arrives.

Living without blueprints restores the **dignity of action taken in uncertainty.** It allows for responsibility without control, commitment without prediction, and meaning without proof. It accepts risk not as a flaw in the system, but as the cost of being human.

STANDING HERE

To live without blueprints is not to abandon reason, systems, or modern life. It is to refuse to mistake them for sources of meaning. It is to stand within limits rather than against them, to act without total explanation, and to accept imperfection without shame.

This posture does not announce itself. It is quiet. It appears in decisions made without audience, in refusals that are not performative, in loyalties maintained without justification, and in judgments exercised even when no framework rewards them.

Beyond the Manufactured Man lies not freedom from systems, but freedom from the illusion that systems can replace judgment, presence, and conscience.

Here is where one stands.

Chapter 25
The Long Arc Recovered

Every age is tempted to believe it stands at a culmination. That its problems are unprecedented, its tools uniquely powerful, and its crises decisive. The modern world, equipped with systems capable of reshaping behavior, coordinating action at scale, and extending life beyond historical expectation, is especially vulnerable to this illusion.

Yet the manufactured man is not the end of the human story. He is a moment within it.

The developments traced in this book did not arise from folly alone. Much of modern life has improved — often dramatically — through the application of rational design, engineering, and institutional coordination. Disease has been reduced. Violence constrained. Knowledge expanded. Material suffering eased. Longevity extended. These are real achievements, not illusions, and they should not be dismissed.

The mistake is not that we gained these things. It is that we mistook them for what was sufficient for a human life.

GAINS WITHOUT DENIAL

The rise of the manufactured man coincided with genuine progress. Systems brought order where chaos had reigned. Procedures replaced arbitrariness. Rights were formalized. Education broadened. Opportunities widened. Many lives are freer, safer, and more secure than at any prior point in history.

To deny these gains would be dishonest.

But gain is never free. Every advance rearranges what is valued, what is neglected, and what is forgotten. When systems improve outcomes, they also shape expectations. When suffering recedes, tolerance for imperfection diminishes. When risk is managed, uncertainty becomes suspect.

What was gained was control. What was lost, gradually, was proportion.

The problem, then, is not that modern systems succeeded — but that their success encouraged an **unexamined expansion of their logic into domains where it no longer fit**.

WHAT WAS LOST QUIETLY

What was lost did not vanish suddenly. It thinned.

Judgment gave way to procedure. Meaning yielded to explanation. Character receded behind compliance. Responsibility became conditional. Completion disappeared. The sense that a life could be lived, judged, and accepted as a whole was replaced by the expectation of continual adjustment.

These losses were not imposed. They were adopted.

The manufactured man did not emerge through conquest alone, but through participation. Systems promised relief from suffering and delivered coordination, efficiency, and safety. In exchange, they asked for alignment — not only outwardly, but inwardly.

Over time, the human scale was obscured. Life became something to manage rather than inhabit. **The long arc of meaning**, once carried through memory, tradition, and judgment, narrowed to the horizon of improvement.

THE LONG ARC STILL HOLDS

Yet beneath the layers of system and correction, the long arc of human life persists.

Across civilizations, eras, and failures, the same irreducible elements remain: judgment under uncertainty, meaning forged through encounter, loyalty maintained without guarantee, conscience that interrupts procedure, and dignity grounded in finitude.

These have survived empires, ideologies, and collapses not because they are efficient, but because they are necessary.

The Enlightenment did not invent reason. The modern age did not invent improvement. The therapeutic turn did not invent care. Each contributed something real. But none replaced the human inheritance that preceded them.

The long arc was not broken. It was obscured.

RECOVERY WITHOUT REVERSAL

To recover the long arc is not to reject the present or retreat into the past. The conditions that shaped earlier forms of meaning cannot be recreated wholesale, nor should they be. What can be recovered is not a world, but a **posture**.

Recovery begins by holding gains without absolutizing them. By using systems without allowing them to define worth. By improving where improvement is fitting and accepting where acceptance is required. By restoring proportion as a governing idea.

This recovery is quiet. It does not announce itself through movements or programs. It appears in the way one stands within limits rather than against them. In the refusal to treat every friction as failure. In the willingness to live unfinished without apology.

What is reclaimed is not certainty, but **continuity**.

LIVING FORWARD IN TIME

The future will bring new systems, new crises, and new temptations to overreach. The manufactured man will not disappear. Engineering will continue. Optimization will advance. None of this is a tragedy.

The question is whether these developments will be held within proportion.

To live forward within the long arc is to resist urgency without drifting into complacency. To act responsibly without demanding guarantees. To accept imperfection without surrendering dignity. To remember that a life need not be perfected to be complete.

Beyond the Manufactured Man lies not a solution, but a scale. Not an answer, but an orientation. Not the end of history, but its continuation.

The arc is longer than we thought.

And it still holds.

CLOSING NOTE

This book has traced how a powerful idea reshaped modern life — and where that idea encountered its limits. It has not offered a blueprint for what comes next, because none is required.

The same conception of the human being that enabled unprecedented advances in coordination, care, and control also shaped the characteristic political pathologies of the modern age. When human nature is treated as fully makeable, politics tends toward root-level redesign — radical solutions and autocratic forms — not necessarily through cruelty or ideology, but through administrative necessity. What begins as improvement hardens into enforcement; what begins as care consolidates into control. Modern radicalism and modern autocracy share a common root: the belief that society, and the human beings within it, can be redesigned without remainder.

Human life has endured across centuries of upheaval, retaining the capacity to recover meaning even when governing frameworks fail. What endures is older, irreducible, and more resilient than any system.

To stand within that inheritance is not to abandon progress, but to **recover perspective**.

That is enough.

Index

181